So Close to
Being the Sh*t,
Y'all Don't
Even Know

SO
CLOSE
TO
BEING
THE
SH*T,

Y'ALL DON'T EVEN KNOW

Retta

ST. MARTIN'S PRESS ⋈ NEW YORK

www.stmartins.com

Designed by Jonathan Bennett

Dedication image created by Freepik

Library of Congress Cataloging-in-Publication Data

Names: Retta author.
Title: So close to being the sh*t, y'all don't even know / Retta.
Other titles: So close to being the shit, y'all don't even know
Description: First edition. I New York : St. Martin's Press, 2018.
Identifiers: LCCN 2017056742 I ISBN 9781250109347 (hardcover) I ISBN 9781250199683 (signed edition) I ISBN 9781250109354 (ebook)
Subjects: LCSH: Retta. I Actors—United States—Biography. I Comedians—United States—Biography. I Conduct of life—Humor.
Classification: LCC PN2287.R445 A3 2018 I DDC 791.4502/8092 [B]—dc23
LC record available at https://lccn.loc.gov/2017056742

Our books may be purchased in bulk for promotional, educational, or business use. Please contact your local bookseller or the Macmillan Corporate and Premium Sales Department at 1-800-221-7945, extension 5442, or by email at MacmillanSpecialMarkets@macmillan.com.

First Edition: May 2018

10 9 8 7 6 5 4 3 2 1

Contents

For my parents, George and Deborah,
the reasons why I am who I am.
To the moon and back.

And for sweet baby Oliver.
Ollie Ollie oxen free.

So Close to Being the Sh*t, Y'all Don't Even Know

Chapter One

Eff You, Effie!

One day in the fall of 2005, I was sitting on my couch, eating Cabaret crackers and watching TV, when I got a call from my manager.

"This is big," he said.

Mmm-hmm. I wasn't falling for that old line. Last time I heard *that*, I was sent to audition for a part on a kids' show . . . with no lines. How do you audition for a part with no lines? Exactly.

"Are you sitting down?"

I *was* sitting down. I'm always sitting down. I'd just bought a used DVD set of *The Shield* and was deep into the corruption of the LAPD Rampart Division. I was on about my 435th episode watching Michael Chiklis, aka The Commish, perpetrate some helluh shady shit. Yo, that show was deep. Rill deep. So, yeah, I was sitting.

"This is *really* big."

Alright. Spit it out already.

"We got you an audition for *Dreamgirls*," he said, then paused for maximum dramatic effect. "The *lead*."

Record scratch. What?

The Tony Award–winning Broadway musical was being

turned into a mainstream movie, and I was being called in to audition for the iconic role of Effie White, the talented but temperamental singer fired from the Dreamettes, an all-girl group that was a thinly veiled version of Motown's The Supremes.

The star-studded cast would be:

Beyoncé. (Shut up.)

Jamie Foxx. (For real?)

Eddie Murphy. (Getttt the fuck outta here!)

And Retta?

Yes, Retta. Why not Retta? This was *the* call I'd been waiting for my whole life; it was the opportunity of a life-time. I was so incredibly grateful and proud, and yet the big-gest feeling I had wasn't excitement. It was dread. And I am telling you, I did not want to go.

Which was insane because I'd always considered myself a pretty fearless person when it came to performing, ever since I'd belted out "Chim Chim Cher-ee" from *Mary Poppins* in a second-grade assembly. I blew the roof off the James Madison Primary School gym in Edison, New Jersey. I hadn't stopped singing since, everything from a high school production of *Anything Goes* to my karaoke go-to, "Killing Me Softly" by The Fugees.* The genre that falls directly into my sweet spot is classical. I've been known to kill some Vivaldi. Still, I was pretty sure, with a little practice, I could sing *Dreamgirls*'s most famous showstopper, "And I Am Telling You, I'm Not Going," with the best of them.

---

* I don't know why the song is credited as "by The Fugees" when Lauryn Hill does all the heavy lifting, but I digress.

But could I hold my own as an actor with the likes of Jamie Foxx and Eddie Murphy and Beyoncé? Firstly, Bey wasn't Queen Bey just yet. She wasn't even Bey yet, really. At the time she was Beyoncé, the lead from Destiny's Child who had just gone solo and had appeared in *The Pink Panther* and *Austin Powers in Goldmember*, neither of which were "dramatic" benchmarks by any stretch of the imagination. This was way before she broke me with *Lemonade*. She's evolved and been through some shit so imagine her performance now! So, no, I wasn't scared to share the screen with the pre-queen.

And, although Eddie is a living legend, the last thing that stuck in my mind about him was the transsexual hooker he got pulled over with. It was prominent in my mind because it happened very near my studio apartment and all I could think was THIS *is where Eddie hangs out?* I *don't hang out around here.* And hey, if that's your jam, then that's your jam. Whatever. But there HAVE to be better pickup locales. After that, Eddie was pretty low-key. Killing it in the voiceover field as Donkey in *Shrek*, but again, he wasn't doing drama.

Jamie Foxx, however, had had a huge hit in *Collateral* with Tom Cruise and then knocked us all out with his Oscar-winning role in *Ray*. So, yeah, THAT may have given me pause, but you know what? That's what the hell I was here for. I came to LA to do my best among the best.

So, no, I wasn't intimidated . . . per se. I'd been a legit working actor for almost ten years, starting at the bottom and working my way up. I got my start in entertainment doing standup at a sorority charity event when I was a junior at Duke University. I had absolutely no idea what I was doing. I just got up there and winged it, regurgitating funny stories my younger brother had told me about himself and his friends. My set killed and my inner attention whore wasn't mad at that crowd approval. For the next four years, I worked as a contract chemist during the day (I'll tell you about that later) and at night did open mics at Goodnight's Comedy Club (also known as Charlie Goodnight's) in Raleigh, North Carolina, one of the top comedy clubs in the United States. I had one goal in mind. I wanted my own sitcom—The Retta Show.

In 1997, I packed my *leased* car* and moved to LA, armed with a stack of unfortunate head shots† and a book titled *Your Film Acting Career.* I auditioned for anything I could and fine-tuned my stand-up.

Your girl husssssstled and that shit paid off. I won Comedy Central's stand-up competition (which later came to be known as the Laugh Riots competition) in '99 and was awarded a brand-new Mercury Cougar, a year's supply of Taco Bell,‡ a spot on Comedy Central's *Premium Blend* and, most important, it led to a spot on the New Faces showcase at the 2000 Montreal Just For Laughs festival. The New Faces showcase was a huge deal because all the television development execs in Hollywood go to see the talent. For a relative Hollywood newbie these credits, along with a costar appearance in *Moe-*

---

* On top of not being allowed to take the car out of state per my lease agreement, I didn't have a job for some time in LA and couldn't afford to pay the bill so it was promptly repossessed.

† To call these head shots unflattering would be an understatement.

‡ It was basically 365 coupons for a free meal at the Bell, and a bitch was broke so I used every last one of 'em. My go-to meal was three tacos with lettuce, extra cheese, sour cream, and a shitload of mild hot sauce and a raspberry iced tea.

sha, appearances in two films, and an HBO pilot, weren't shabby.

Moesha is one of three all-black projects I've ever booked . . . in my career . . . to this day, and I think that partially fed into my fear about the *Dreamgirls* audition. This was an iconic piece of black theater. I call it black theater because even though it wasn't written by black authors it was mostly an African American cast depicting R&B acts of the 1960s and '70s. And as my manager kept pointing out, it was going to be Big. At the time, I felt like I didn't really fit into the black comedy scene. I told myself I wasn't urban enough in my act. I just wasn't covering the same subject matter that I saw other black comics doing. I didn't write about growing up in the projects, smoking weed, or my epic sexcapades—not that I had any. That wasn't my shit and, as a result, I feared the black audience for a long time.

I remember doing a set at the Phat Tuesdays show at The Improv and I was scared to death because I didn't know if I'd be embraced by a black crowd. I was one of those girls who the black girls in my high school said sounded "white." Everybody knows you can live or die on a black comedy stage. I didn't think they would like me, because I wasn't doing quintessentially black material. It took me a long time to learn that as long as you're yourself that audience will accept you. You transcend it. There are white comics who do black shows and kill. As long as you're yourself, and you're funny . . . you're good. *Dreamgirls* being a "black" classic could serve as my vehicle into the hearts of the black audience. It seemed the safest bet because I wouldn't be playing myself, I'd be playing a character. A beloved character. An iconic character in the

black theater canon. Giving me the chance to finally be recognized by the black audience.

My original goal was to be a sitcom star. Now I was being
offered an opportunity to be a movie star? Yeah, a movie star.
But first I'd have to get through the audition. I'd have to prove
I was the perfect Effie to a roomful of producers, casting
agents, and the director, Bill Condon—who just happened to
be the Academy Award–nominated writer of the film adap-
tation of *Chicago*. I'd have to sing "And I Am Telling You, I'm
Not Going." Probably a capella. For them to *hear*. With their
ears. Now if that doesn't make you want to shit your pants,
I don't know what will. I practiced in the shower 100 times
100 different ways, but that couldn't prepare me for the real
deal. As many times as I had auditioned in my career, I still
felt sick every time. This would be infinitely worse. Why?
Because this was going to be Big. That motherfucker was in
my head.

The fear of rejection is real, my friends. When you've had
your fair share of soul-crushing, self-esteem-destroying experiences, it'll do a serious number on your psyche. Here's one
for the record books: A famous female TV writer-producer,
who had created a beloved all-female sitcom in the '80s, was
ALL about me after I auditioned for her new pilot. She decided I wasn't right for THAT part but wanted to create something for me. Every six months, she'd check in with me and ask
if I was available. *Um, yes, I'm available! I'm never not available
for you!* She'd come up with a show idea for HBO about an
all-female vice squad in downtown LA and was I interested?
After I immediately said yes, she told me the character was a
lesbian.

"She's hardcore. I think you'd be great."

Okay, just give me a job! That's what I wanted to say. But before I could, I panicked. This was cable. HBO. Lots of nek-kidness.

"I gotta say, I haven't done a lot of things on camera, so I've never had a sex scene on camera. I've never even kissed a man on camera so I definitely haven't been skin on skin with a woman. I can't show my tits and I can't lick anyone else's. I think I can handle kissing a woman but that's about it."

"Oh, you'd never have to do *all* that!"

She was right because the vice thing didn't see the light of day. Instead, she decided she wanted to do a dramedy about a wealthy Texas family and called me up again with the pitch, which was also being developed for HBO. "Their housekeeper who lived with them forever had a daughter and they loved her so much, they sent her to college and law school and now she's the attorney for the family. That's your part!"

"Word? Okay."

"She's a lesbian. And her name is Retta."

"You really tryna make me a lesbian, huh? I'm down. Let's do this."

I had already shot a pilot for HBO called *$5.15/Hour.** The suits at HBO were nervous. *Sex and the City* was ending and they were looking for another hit. They had high hopes for two promising projects: *$5.15/Hour* and another pilot called *Entourage.* "*Entourage* doesn't look that great," the execs on

---

* *$5.15/Hour* is where I met my friend America Ferrera, TV's *Ugly Betty.* We spent a little over two weeks shooting the pilot in Austin. It was written by Rodney Rothman and directed by Richard Linklater. It was a great time and we were all sad it didn't make it onto the HBO schedule.

$5.15/Hour snickered. "It'll never go." I'll give you one guess as to which made it to air and which didn't. Even though my show didn't go, the suits knew me, liked me, and had said as much, so when this producer pitched me as the lesbian family lawyer I knew I was in like Flynn. Or so I thought. It turned out I was gonna have to audition for the part. The part she'd *created* just for me. The character she naaaaamed Retta. Apparently, one of the casting directors had her doubts about me and needed to see me read. I agreed to go in, but now I was helluh nervous. After that first audition the writer-producer called me to tell me they wanted the director to meet with me. We would talk about the part and I would come back to do another producer's session.

After that second audition, the producer called me. "I can't believe I have to make this call . . ." she started but didn't need to finish. I didn't get the part. It was the most heartbreaking rejection I'd had since I'd arrived in Hollywood. Tossed back into the ocean of actors, like a rotting boot on a fishing line, I kept checking IMDb to see if they kept the character's name as "Retta." I was prepared to die a thousand deaths if they had but thankfully they did end up changing the name. Plus, it never aired.

I'd like to say this was the acting Gods lookin' out for a bitch, but sadly, this kind of thing happens ALL the time. I had a friend named Wendy get fired from her own show named *Wendy* and someone else was hired to play Wendy. Let THAT shit roll around in your cerebellum for a second. Fucking brutal.

Even a full year after the rejection, it's hard not to give up when nightmares like that happen. You're bitter, broken, and usually BROKE. But just when you're about to throw in the towel, something like *Dreamgirls* rolls in. Every time you try to get out, they pull you back in! A week had passed since my manager first gave me the great news that the *Dreamgirls* producers wanted to see me, but I still hadn't set up a time for an audition.

"We really want you to go in for this!" he begged again.

All I could say was, "That's crazy."

This was my big chance and I was blowing it. Was I in shock? What was happening? What was wrong with me?

I could sing, I could act, but even more than the fear of rejection and judgment from the black audience, there were two things crucial to a lead role, like Effie White, in a period musical still holding me back and giving me massive anxiety. For one, I couldn't dance. Back up, back up. I CAN dance. I love to dance and I know I gots moves cuz when I used to break shit down at parties folks would be like dammmmmmn. I don't know if it was because they were surprised that a big girl could dance, but people were always impressed with my skeelz. When I used to go to clubs in college I didn't need somebody to ask me to dance. I was there to WORK, to work that floor. We did all the dances, the Monster Wop, the Butterfly, the Tootsie Roll, the Cabbage Patch, the Biz. I would do the Reebok but would incorporate the pause and the robot turn from left to right.* Whaaaaaaat?

Every year for my birthday party, I hire a DJ and there are two separate rooms. The bar room and the dance floor.

---

* I'm dating myself by naming these old-ass dances but I feel y'all need to KNOW. I was doin' the damn thing.

I make sure everyone knows the dance floor is for DANCE.
ING. "Don't come in here if you're not gonna dance. Don't
waste the space. Do not come up in here unless you're ready to
bring it." I believe that 75 percent of dancing is facial expression and that's another reason why I think I appeared so good
at it. Very few people can compete with my facial skills. I'm
not a professional dancer, I don't have any formal dance train-
ing, but I did tap and dance numbers in high school produc-
tions. I was a quick study when it came to choreography.

So, in conclusion, I CAN dance. I'm just not physically able
to do choreography anymore. I have two knee injuries from
junior high and college, and a messed-up ankle from an accident at a Hollywood party. Right after I got to LA, I went
to a shindig at a house in the Hills. I didn't want to go, I was
in a stank mood, but my friend insisted. The place was packed.
I poured myself a drink and about forty seconds after I stepped
out onto the deck, the deck collapsed. I dropped about five
feet and dozens of people fell on top of me. I was on the
bottom of the pile with a dislocated ankle. After everybody
stopped screaming and finally got up, a kid who looked like
he was rushing Kappa Sigs stood over me.

"It looks like your ankle's dislocated. We need to reduce
your ankle!" he screamed frantically. "I can do it! I'm a med
student at UCLA!" His halitosis was sponsored by Maker's
Mark and I wasn't about to be his practice dummy.

"WE don't need to do shit. And I'm gonna need YOU to
back the fuck away from me."

The fire department finally came and a few handsome fellas
saved me. They strapped me to a long backboard and carried
me out of the yard like a swollen Cleopatra. The night left me

with a pair of ruined jeans, an outrageous hospital bill, and a fucked-up ankle for the rest of my life. How was I gonna dance in *Dreamgirls* with a wonky ankle and a pair of busted knees? I pictured myself asking the director for too many breaks and asking a resentful production assistant for too many ice packs, thus ending up the set "diva" who had all of four credits to her name. I didn't want to get a reputation as a pain in the ass.

Second, the idea of wardrobe was freaking me out. I knew all those girls in The Dreamettes would have to dress alike and I was scared they wouldn't be able to find matching dresses in my size. I was so green to the filmmaking scene that I didn't know the costume department would just MAKE us all the same dress. My neophyte ass thought they were going to Nordstrom to shop for a period piece. I was also panicked that I'd have to wear heels. I don't wear heels. I can't. I *have* to wear completely flat shoes at all times because of the pain and scar tissue in my ankle.

I was clueless and I'd created this whole story in my head of how it was gonna go down. I convinced myself I couldn't survive the shoot, a shoot I hadn't yet been asked to join. A film I hadn't even auditioned for yet.

I was sure I couldn't do it.

So I didn't do it.

I never said no; I was way more chickenshit than that. I just kept avoiding it, putting it off. For about three months I never made myself available, and it got to the point where they had a movie to cast and so they did. They went with the seventh-place finalist of season three of *American Idol*. They cast Jennifer Hudson. She had no credits. But you know what she *did* have? The balls to show up to the audition.

When it was official that I wouldn't be auditioning because the role was cast, I wasn't relieved. I was ashamed of myself. For the first time in my life, I understood the phrase "the fear of success." Before then I always thought it was the dumbest thing I'd ever heard. But now I got it. Because *THAT* was what I wanted. To be in those big movies with big stars. That's why I was here. But I was scared. Scared of things not going perfectly. Scared of being perceived as a problem. Scared of sharing the screen with big names. Basically scared of success.

The next Christmas, I went to see *Dreamgirls* with my brother back home in New Jersey. He didn't know that I'd been offered an audition for Effie. I didn't tell anyone. When the lights went down, and I saw Jennifer Hudson on the big screen for the first time as Effie, I looked down at her feet.

She was wearing flats. The kind you can fold and put in your purse.*

Mother. Fucker.

I have no doubt, I could have sung "And I Am Telling You, I'm Not Going." I don't know that I'd have sung it better than Jennifer. She won an Academy Award for Best Supporting Actress based on that performance. What I do know, if I can get Franklin D. Roosey here, is that I let the fear of fear itself get the best of me. Jennifer hadn't done jack before that movie but she had the confidence within herself to take a risk that paid off big-time.

I did not win an Oscar but I learned a valuable lesson that

---

* Full disclosure: She did wear medium heels in some group scenes but the scene where she sang "And I Am Telling You, I'm Not Going," the Oscar-winning scene, homegirl had on flats.

stays with me to this day and plays on a loop in my head any-
time I have a big audition. It goes a little something like this:

*Bitch, stop wasting time fearing the worst. Living through the
worst is never as hard as fearing it. Fight the fear and go do what
you gotta do. That's what you came here for.*

Chapter Two

The Darkest of Magic

"I used to think an addict was someone who lived on the far edges of society. Wild-eyed, shaven head and living in a filthy squat. That was until I became one."

—random quote from a meme I found
in Google images

Hi, my name is Retta and I'm an addict. What am I addicted to? Juuust about everything, but shopping and eating are at the top of the list. I hoard DVDs. I own way more handbags than one person needs. I've never met a short rib I didn't like. I have too many shampoos, hair gels, and face lotions. Coffee mugs. Sneakers. Cardigans. Flip-flops and coats. Those last two are quite the juxtaposition, considering you rarely wear one with the other.

You know, I have such an addictive, obsessive personality, it's kind of a miracle I didn't end up on *Celebrity Rehab*. Dr. Drew would've had a field day with me. "Why the flip-flops AND the overcoats, Retta?" But something always held me back from getting too hooked on the REALLY fucked-up things out there. When I was in high school, I was such a Goody

Two-shoes I walked home from a high school party thrown by the most popular guy in school because a lot of the kids were drinking. The first time I DID try alcohol, in college, mind you, I was so naïve about it that I thought I was drunk after one drink. I wasn't. I was just sweating.

I was about that straight-arrow life. I didn't just say no to drugs, I vehemently refused to take ANY kind of pill whatsoever. Not even for my period. For years I suffered from excruciating cramps, until my friend pointed out the irony of my working for a giant pharmaceutical firm and having a fear of pharmaceutical drugs and urged me to at least try Ibuprofen. I did and oh my God, the FUCK was I thinking? So many lost weekends. Countless evenings lying on the couch with a cold towel on my head and a heating pad across my belly when I could've been at the mall eating Friendly's sundaes and gossiping about the JV football players. I can never get that time back.

Don't get it twisted, mamma found her way to that sweet nectar of the Gods eventually. I had quite a spirit for the spirits. I started late but I made up for lost time. My first few years in LA I used to tear shit up. On the spectrum from Dean Martin to Gary Busey, I lingered closer to Dino, as I am a stealthy lush. I kept my intoxication, as they say, on the low-low. But the drinking period of my life didn't last long and I moved on to other habitual behavior. And before you start setting your DVRs for my episode of *Behind the Music* (do they even make those anymore? Is VH1 still a channel?), my addictions are pretty lame . . . I mean tame. Like, just this last year, I gave in to temptation and turned to the dark side—

the dark roast side! Suddenly, at the age of forty-xfsjklzv, I developed an addiction to coffee.

I'd gotten one of those fancy Keurig home brewing machines FREE in an Emmy swag bag. Top of the line. My bestie couldn't stop talking about it and how she couldn't believe they just gave 'em to us. I didn't drink coffee. I had not succumbed to the spell that so many Angelenos had found themselves under. I was like, *whatever.* This free piece of establishment machinery didn't move me. I'd already gotten a coffeemaker as a wrap gift one year from *Parks and Recreation.* That thing sat on my kitchen floor for yeeeears, ignored like a white crayon. What was so special about this Keurig? My friend all but threatened me to try the damn thing. So I did, and I'll never be the same.

Whosever idea it was to give those things out is a genius and deserves a seat on the board of Keurig, cuz they got me. I'm all-in. The names of the different flavors alone were enough to pique my interest. Black Tiger, Mahogany, Jet Fuel. Jet Fuel? Yeah, Jet. Fuel. Flavors like Cinnabon Classic Cinnamon Roll or The Original Donut Shop—which literally smells like you're walking into a 7-Eleven early in the morning (in the good way)—made me nostalgic for the days when we stopped at the corner store for Now and Laters and Jolly Rancher Stix before school.

But it was Dark Magic that changed my life 4Ever. Once I had my first sip, there was no going back. I don't know how to describe it other than it suddenly made me feel like I was doing things right. Like when you learn how to ride your bike or tie your shoe. At first you're slow and awkward and have to talk your way through it with the Bunny poem: *Over, under, around and through. Meet Mr. Bunny Rabbit, pull and through.* But then one day you just do it. That's how it was for me with Dark Magic. Before Dark Magic I was figuring out how to exist in the world and after Dark Magic I was just doing it.

Where had Dark Magic been my whole life? I'd been in blissful ignorance of this delightful subculture, even though it's probably in my genes to be a coffee nut. My mom has always been addicted—to the point she got a UTI from her daily use of Sweet'N Low in every cup—and it made zero sense to me. Just. Didn't. Get it. Why does she like coffee so much? Can you even call it coffee? She drinks generic instant, for God's sake. I didn't even drink coffee back then and knew that shit was trash, but she was all about it. That was the marker for my acute case of coffeenoma.

But now I'm a proud member of the coffee cult, and I've fully committed to my new lifestyle. I love the futuristic equipment, the accessories, the mugs! So many fun mugs, I don't even know where to put them all. Mugs with my picture. Whimsical mugs. Holiday mugs. Mugs that say "World's Best Entry-Level Employee." Free mugs from drug companies. College mugs. Sooo many college mugs.*

I love coffee, and if you know anything else about me, you know I love social media.† I have made coffee a centerpiece in my social media presence. More specifically, Dark Magic

---

* When I toured the college circuit I was often given a mug as a gift from the school's programming committee.

† You're more likely to know I'm one half of the "Treat Yo Self" team but that's another chapter.

is ALL OVER my Snapchat. It's where I first admitted to the world that my name is Retta and I'm a javaholic. And to think, I used to HATE on people who constantly posted coffee on their Instagram and Twitter feeds, rolling my eyes while scrolling quickly past each post. I'd even been tempted to un-follow, so strong was my opinion. I have a friend who used to post her cup-a-joe pics EVERY SINGLE DAY. Not even in inter-esting mugs, or at least with latte art of a leaf or Jesus or a simple heart on top. I mean, give us *somethin'* to look at. Nope. Just a generic Starbucks cup with her name spelled wrong. Even worse, it always included at least ten hashtags, some that related to coffee, like #coffee, #brew, #caffeineislife, and some that had nothing to do with coffee, like #blessed or #riseandgrind—which technically *could* be about coffee but I know it wasn't. *Let it go, girl,* I thought. *It's not that serious!* Now I want to send my friend a formal letter of apology and present her with a $1,000 Starbucks gift card. I get it. I'm her. I'm every woman and man who loves coffee and wants to shout it out loud and proud from the rooftops to their Snap-chat story! And I do.

My Snapchat followers know that every morning, I post a video of my first cup of coffee, as I gleefully sing, "Dark Maaagiiic!" Can't stop, won't stop. So much so that since starting my coffee routine, my once relatively pearly whites ain't so white no mo'. At my last dentist appointment, the hygienist looked in my mouth and frowned. "Why are your teeth brown?" she asked, puzzled.

"Oh man. I started drinking coffee."

"Ugggghhhhhhhh," she moaned. Coffee is the dental professional's worst nightmare. Well, that and the lack of flossing, which I don't get cuz I floss. Like a lot. Almost too much. I didn't say anything, because she was two knuckles deep in my mouth. But I was thinking, *Figure it out, homie. It's not just part of my life now, it is my life now. So figure it ooouuutttt.*

Then she proceeded to beat the shit out of my teeth.

Hey, I deserved it and I owned it. That's the price you pay when you're committed to a cause. I admit, coffee's a fairly new passion, and there was a steep learning curve. I figured out some things the hard way. Like the feeling of "I swear to God if anybody pisses me off before I have my first cup" in the a.m. wasn't really me having a heart attack; that the stank breath most associated with office workers and construction foremen is due to coffee; and, oh yes, most important, the POOPING. Nobody warned me about the pooping! It is both a blessing and a curse.

Early in my coffee career I made the mistake of getting a Frappuccino at the airport right before a four-hour flight. I have never regretted anything more. I had a window seat and was in big trouble right away. I had to keep getting up and it was so embarrassing. There's nothing more humbling than pooping in the tightest of bathrooms, knowing people are waiting right outside the door. Then I had to fight my way back to my seat, make the people get up and barrel my way to my spot as gracefully as a big girl can in coach, bending back the tops of the seats in the row in front of me and getting mad side-eye from the other sardines. Then, as soon as I sat down, almost immediately, I got that bubble-gut rumble again. *Dear God. Please. Why? What did I do to deserve this?* I'm sorry, folks, but I'm gonna need you to get up again. *Now.*

That, I was mad about. But once I figured out the pooping-coffee science, and that different blends had different timing (for example, Dark Magic *works* its magic exactly an hour after drinking it), it was a revelation. I keeps it movin'! I can start my day! Hallelujah! Then I was able to schedule my life accordingly. Do I drink that set coffee before hair and makeup, or am I gonna need to hold out until after hair but before makeup? If I drink a Frappuccino, am I able to spend most of the day in the comfort of my own home because it's gonna be awhile? If I know exactly what's going to happen, I'm solid. If I don't, I'm anxious and have that running commentary in my head. *How do I time this? Is it worth it? Why are you making a big deal of this? Everybody poops!* It doesn't matter that everybody poops. They WILL talk SHIT about you . . . literally.

Here's one thing I *don't* get. How all those girls in their lululemons at the gym drink coffee while working out. They're on the treadmill *with* the friggin' Starbucks, just shaking it all up in their stomachs. I'm assuming it gives them a high and thus they feel energized to do the run, but if I'm gonna shit my pants on the treadmill at the Hollywood Y, I don't know that it's worth it.

I'm not gonna lie, I love the high. I'm like a meth-head getting shit DONE, overly fixated on my variety of pods. I just can't help sharing my love of my most beloved blend on my Snapchat. I gotta spread the good word. "Daarrrrrrrk Maaagiiic!" I singsong. Or I commiserate: "God help anyone who *gets* on my fucking *nerves* before I have my coffee!"

"I feel you! I feel you!" they Snap back.

I'm almost a cult leader—is that bad? It's gotten to the

point that people are sending me messages that they're addicted to Dark Magic, too, and can't start their day unless they hear my Dark Magic jingle. I'm drunk with java power.

The only downside to all this—besides the beige teeth and construction foreman breath—is that I also get tweets and Snaps saying I'm single-handedly destroying the earth with the pods, which are filling up the garbage dumps. "Retta, you really shouldn't be using K-Cups!" they scold, sending me links to all sorts of environmental sites.

Ugh.

I do feel guilty and I do promise to look into an alternative. But for now, I must ignore those messages. I'm so sorry. This is where I'm at. I might as well be smacking my forearm trying to find that one good vein because I'm in deep. I've become that person who can't go to work without bringing my own creamer. And not just any creamer. It's gotta be International Delight Hazelnut coffee creamer. Not Coffeemate. Not Dunkin' Donuts. INTERNATIONAL DELIGHT. Not Butterscotch. Not Vanilla. HAZELNUT.

I know that I might have a problem, but I'm not ready to face it yet. If it's a choice between coffee or crack, I'm goin' with Dark Magic. I don't know what to tell you. I need it.

Top 10 Technology Truthisms*

1. The jobless spend the most time on Snapchat.

2. Astronauts can tweet from space but I can't get my Wi-Fi to reach my bedroom.

3. I experience anxiety when I haven't updated my Bitmoji's outfit to be season-appropriate.

4. I don't care how "advanced" we're supposed to be. I'll give you my cordless landline when you pry it from my cold, dead hands.

5. When I get an alert that a friend has *JUST* joined Instagram: 😵😵😵😵😵.

6. How do we not have voice-activated search on TiVo? So much button pressing. What are we, animals??

7. No one cares about ur Snapchat concert vids. We get it. You're *THERE*, we're not. Enjoy the show & stop tryna make us jelly w/ ur grainy footage.

8. I once stole a fan's selfie & cropped her out cuz the light was perf on moi.

9. When I see someone using a pay phone I immediately think a heist is about to go down cuz who the F uses pay phones anymore?

10. I unfollow friends on Instagram because they post too many "inspirational" quotes. Just let me have my shitty day.

---

* This is the first of the obligatory lists I was told should be added to a book of essays.

Chapter Three

From Roaches to Riches, Bitches!

The other day my publicist had to book me a last-minute flight to Cabo San Lucas so I could join my friends on a vacation that I had JUST found out I had the time in my schedule to go on. She checked Orbitz, Expedia, Travelocity, and KAYAK, every dark corner of the internet, and called me with bad news. There was cause for panic. The only seats available were in coach. WHAT?? No first-class seats? I haven't flown coach in like, three years. I started flipping out, like, a for real and for true anxiety attack, and actually thought about canceling. Then this internal monologue played in my head:

"Really, bitch? You can't sit in coach for two and a half hours? Settle the fuck down. You lived off American cheese and Top Ramen for a good two years and ate cockroaches when you were a kid. I think you can humble yourself and manage a coach flight to the south of Mexico."

Okay, now you all relax. It was one roach and I wasn't fed the thing. I don't need folks approaching my parents about how they raised their kids. The cockroach thing was an accident. When I was a baby, my parents lived in a two-bedroom apartment in the projects in Newark, New Jersey, and, yes, our building had cockroaches. Like before you went in a room, you'd have to turn on the light switch, wait a moment while they all scattered and ran for cover, then you could enter. I mean you didn't HAVE to wait. Maybe you live the kind of life where you feel the need to confront a room full of roaches, but that's not the life we lived.

Anyway, when I was about seven months old, I was crawling around the apartment. My mother says she saw me stop to look at something but my diaper-covered bottom was all she could see. She saw me sit back as I brought my hand to my mouth. As she darted toward me to stop me from partaking in a dead cockroach, I popped it in my little mouth before she could get to me. She was horrified. As. Was. I!, as I heard this story when I was older and could comprehend the severity of the situation.

"I was screaming as I tried to fish it out of your mouth," she told me with a sick look on her face.

"Did you get it?" I asked, so scared of what the answer was going to be. And, with the same sick look on her face, she shook her head. So there you have it. I ate a roach, people.

What I'm trying to say is that I come from humble beginnings, so I don't know who I thought I was, refusing to fly coach. I flew ONE time on a private jet with Glenn Close and her dog, and now I'm too good to slum it in steerage? Bitch, you *come* from steerage! Some might say we were poor while others might prefer to label us low-income. I'll just say we weren't wealthy.

My dad, George Sr., and my mom, Deborah, immigrated

to the United States from the African country of Liberia so my mom could go to college. My dad got a job in the Revlon warehouse and my mom worked as an insurance adjuster while in school, but with three kids (my younger brothers, George Jr. and Michen, and me) and a revolving group of cousins living with us, we were always broke.

My dad was blue-collar before he retired and my mother would be considered pink-collar. We never had money to spare. A phrase I often heard growing up was "money is tight" and another (not so diplomatic) one was "money doesn't grow on trees."

My father was a diligent "saver" and once he had enough for a down payment he bought us a beat-up house in Cliffwood Beach, a Jersey suburb less than an hour from New York City. At first I didn't want to move. I was a freshman in high school and had just made the cheerleading team. I didn't want to move away from my friends. But I thought it might be okay because we were each going to get our own room. I didn't have to share with my two brothers and cousin anymore (yeah, there were FOUR of us in that room). I wouldn't have to sleep on a bunk bed anymore. I would get a big-girl bed. I was getting my parents' old bed but whatevs, I wasn't gonna have to jump three feet to use the bathroom in the middle of the night like some parkour hipster. I was going to be able to say "my house" and not mean "a two-bedroom apartment that housed six." It was going to be an *actual* house.

Before we get into the house, I should probably explain how it was we had an apartment of six when I only had two brothers. First, let me introduce you to them. There's George, who is four years younger than me, and Mich, who's eleven years younger. I am pretty close to both now but growing up, not so much. Starting when I was around nine years old, my mother used to force me to hang out with George. She made me take him whenever I was leaving the house to go play. I haaaaaaated it. Who the hell wants to hang out with their little brother? My friends weren't that into it either. I already shared a room with the little thorn in my side and now I had to share my quality friend time as well. Total bullshit.

When I was about twelve years old I got the chicken pox. I was stuck in our apartment for two weeks with nothing to do . . . but spend time with my brother. It was maddening. So when I was finally over the pox I was elated to be allowed to get out of prison (our apartment) and hang with my friends. On my way out the door on my first day of freedom my mother said, "Take your brother!" *Whaaaaa? Come. On!* So as not to get the stink eye I reluctantly let my brother accompany me to the park. As we were leaving the building I noticed he had a small bump on his neck and one on his arm and one near his ear. Holy shit! "George, I think you have chicken pox!" We walked back upstairs and showed my mother. She confirmed that he indeed had the pox. *Yes!!!!!* I skipped out of the apartment to meet my friends . . . solo. I had two weeks of brother-free playground time ahead of me. It was glorious.

When George was old enough to have his own friends from school I got a bit of a reprieve from playing his in-house cruise director. But he continued to bug. He and his friends would record themselves talking on a tape recorder and they'd use MY tapes. Tapes that had songs I had recorded from the radio after waiting forever for stations to play them. They'd record right in the MIDDLE of songs I loved. And they just recorded themselves talking . . . about NOTHING. Nobody gave a shit what Hot Wheels they lost from last Christmas. Nobody cared how many boys were in their gym class compared to how many girls there were. Nobody cared that Friday was their favorite day at school because it was Pizza Day. But the most egregious of offenses took place one day after school when I was in sixth grade. It was the year that Kenny Linyard (name changed to protect the innocent) moved to Edison, New Jersey. He was super cute and my friends and I alllll had crushes on him. We talked about him on the phone every day for a week when he moved to town. After spending a good deal of time extolling the prepubescent attributes of Kenny Linyard, I was walking past the bedroom we shared with our cousin when I heard my brother talking on the phone. I heard him saying something along the lines of "Hey, so and so, do you have a brother named Kenny? I think my sister and her friends like him. They talk about some kid named Kenny Linyard on the phone every day after school." I went ballistic. I pounced on him with the fury of a thousand suns. I pounded him until my mother came in screaming for me to stop. My poor mother. It really used to leave her weary when we didn't get along.

My brother continued to be annoying through high school. Walking into my room without knocking. Touching my stuff when I was nothing but clear about him NOT touching my stuff. It wasn't until I was away at college that we started to like each other. We talked on the phone when I called home and it was during these calls that I learned that my brother George was actually kinda funny. As it turns out, he's the funniest one in our family. I now enjoy spending time with my brother . . . for the most part. Probably cuz I'm not obligated to do it.

My youngest brother, Mich, short for Michen, which was my grandfather's name, is the baby of the family. So, needless to say, he experienced the most favored of childhoods. I like to think it's because my mother just no longer had the energy to put up with the stubbornness of Sirleaf children. For example, I was left at the dinner table and not allowed to leave until I was finished eating (I slept there on more than one occasion). George was only required to eat the parts of dinner he liked but Michen was made a separate meal cuz he was soooo particular. I never went to camp. George went to day camp and Mich got to go to sleepaway camp. The one thing my mother did try to do differently and for the better with her smallest little was keep him away from sugar. George and I were sugar fiends. My mom would buy no-name cornflakes because . . . financial hardship, so George and I would saturate them in an obscene amount of sugar because (1) no-name cornflakes were nasty and (2) we used evaporated milk and never got the ratio of milk to water right, so it was always a bit on the sour side. Copious amounts of sugar offset said sour.

Mich was never given sugar. Neither in his hot nor cold cereal. We think he was predisposed to a sugar addiction. Once, when he was about three years old, he walked into the kitchen with blue lips. When my cousin called him over to investigate she noticed his tongue was blue, too. When she asked him what happened, his "Nothing" response made her eyes water. Not because it was sad but because the menthol on his breath was so strong everyone in the kitchen could smell it. It turned out that he had gotten into her nightstand where she kept her Halls cough drops and eaten every single one in the new bag. But because three-year-olds aren't all that smart, he put all the wrappers in the garbage can next to the nightstand. This incident should have been the forewarning of things to come.

Since Mich was not used to sugar, George and I decided to blow his mind one morning. My parents had left for work and we were home before school. I made Mich his cereal and George snuck in sugar when Mich wasn't looking. We watched as he took his first spoonful. At first he was perplexed because something was different. He ate another and another and with each spoonful he grew more and more delighted. He finally said, "What's in this?" and we told him sugar. BIG MISTAKE. From then on Mich made me and George look like amateurs when it came to a love of/need for sucrose. He snuck it into his cereal every day. He soon started getting his fix in church, where he would sidle up to every elderly parishioner, smile his cute smile, and walk away with a Werther's Original caramel or a Pep O Mint Life Saver. By the time he got in the car to go home, he was lousy with hard *and* chewy candy.

To this day my baby brother is picky about his food and loves him some sweets. And you know what's perfect? He married a woman who can bake her ass off. Even crazier, she enjoys going to WrestleMania with him. Oh, did I not mention my brother is STILL into professional wrestling? Yeah. Big-time. At their wedding reception, the tables were named after WWF Superstars of Wrestling. I was at the Rowdy Roddy Piper table. They even hired pro-wrestling ring announcer Howard Finkel to announce the wedding party. Those wrestling nerds lost their damn minds. Personally I don't get it but you love what you love. I have my patent leather Louis Vuitton Alma bags, he has his wrestling belts. Oh, did I forget to mention my brother owns wrestling belts? Yeah. God bless his wife, April.

As for my "cousin" sitch, growing up we always had cousins living with us. My first cousin to live with us, we'll call her "S," moved in when we lived in the two-bedroom apartment. She came to the States from Liberia when my mom was close to giving birth to my youngest brother. She was out of high school and was coming to help with the new baby. She was our version of an au pair. She shared a room with me and my brother, so trust me when I say it was tight quarters. At first it was weird but we grew used to it. One cuzzo, no big, right? When we moved to the house it felt like, *yasssss everyone gets their own room.* We had seven WHOLE bedrooms to choose from. It was on like Donkey Kong, yo! I had a room, my brother George had a room, and my cousin S shared a room with the baby, whom she took care of. My parents turned one of the rooms into a study/music room, one was kept as a guest room, and the last was used mainly for storage.

It wasn't long before my mom's cousin "V" moved in with her young daughter, Li'l M. They set up camp in the guest room. Some years later cousin "Q" from my dad's side of the family moved in. She was the same age as my baby brother. Dad moved the storage items to the study/music room and basement and put cousin Q in there. So let's review: two parents, three kids, and cousins S, Q, V, and Li'l M. That's nine people spread among six available bedrooms. Oh, did I mention that my mom's godmother also came from Liberia and stayed with us for a few months (in my room) and then when

I left for college cousin Q's older grown-ass sister,* who was a hot freaking mess, also came to stay because *her* mother couldn't deal with her? The fuck? The one good thing about that sitch was that my mother would not allow anyone else to move into my room. Cousin Crazy rested her head on the daybed in the upstairs sitting room, so when I came home for the holidays I had somewhere to hide out from the madness of the Sirleaf Halfway House for Wayward Fam.

Aaaaaaaanyway, I remember pulling up to the house and thinking the yard wasn't like the yards I'd seen in front of the houses we'd passed on the bus ride to school. It was barely green because it barely had any grass. Just yellowy patches of what used to be grass and dirt. But I thought, *At least it's big.* I remember walking in and immediately grabbing my nose. It reeked of animal feces, which we later found out was because the previous owners, who were in their seventies, had dogs that hadn't left the house for years. I was mortified that we were going to live in this disaster area but my father was so proud. This was his HOUSE. This was OUR "new" house.

As I mentioned, there were seven bedrooms, so it was definitely huge and, after living on top of each other for so long, this was at least a welcome change. My dad and his buddy, his ace and loyal handyman Caesar, began renovations on day one, ripping up the rancid carpets,† painting, and the like.

---

* She was crazy as a loon. She'd sometimes walk around the house topless, which freaked my brothers out, and my parents had to go off on her. Eventually she created more drama than it was worth, and we all decided she probably shouldn't stay.

† Yeah, there was carpeting in a home where dogs hadn't left the house for more than two years. Try to imagine how foul they were.

That was twenty-seven years ago and they have been working on it as a team ever since. If you saw it now, I think you'd be impressed with my parents' house. My mother has done one hell of a job decorating. You might wonder if she needs quite that many pillows on the couches. And the sheer number of knickknacks might be jarring at first glance, but all in all, I think you'd be impressed.

Back then, though, I never thought I was poor. I knew we weren't rich, but I had no clue we were poor. To me, it was perfectly normal that I got a free lunch at school. I mean, how cool is FREE lunch? There was no shame in my free-lunch game. I had no idea there *should* be. It's not like anyone ever pointed it out to me. It was normal to us that everything in our cupboards was the all-white generic brand. I mean I was borderline OCD and everything was uniform so I loved it. We didn't have Kellogg's Frosted Flakes. We had regulah ol' corn flakes. We never had whole milk, just cans of evaporated milk. When we ran out of that we used non-dairy creamer for our cereal, and when we ran out of THAT we'd just eat cereal with water. Tap. Water. On generic corn flakes. *Mmm-mmmm* <<makes a not-so-*Mmmmmm* face>>, sugar water with a crunch. The real tragedy of growing up in a low-income household is that I never had a proper Oreo cookie until college. We were relegated to the cheaper Hydrox brand, which sounds like an industrial-strength toilet-bowl cleaner, not a cookie. We always had giant cheap bags of rice—a Liberian staple—and bread. A Taystee Bakery outlet was right up the road, so when they had day-old sales, my mom would fill up an entire shopping cart for ten dollars and we'd freeze it.

Deborah Sirleaf lived that "waste not want not" life. She

taught us to squeeze toothpaste from the very bottom so that we used every bit of it. When we finished a tube of lotion she would cut the bottom off then cut down the sides so that we could get that last bit of moisturizer out of it. My mother had a pail under the bathroom sink where she would store the last bits of bar soap. Once it filled up, she would use the little pieces to make large bars of soap. And since we normally bought whatever soap was on sale, there were different brands and different colors in that pail. Our homemade soap looked like a pastel patchwork bar. It was the soap version of a quilt.

I got all my clothes for school from discount superstores, but I didn't realize they were cheap. I'll never forget the time I was to attend my sixth grade dance. My mother took me to Kmart and we found this cream-colored sateen dress with a cream lace overlay. I thought it was soooo gorgeous. I absolutely loved it. I never thought twice about the fact that we got it at a Kmart. It was pretty, I looked good in it, and I just knew I was the shit. We later stepped things up and started hitting up Marshalls for my gear. That place was so cool. They had brands I had heard kids mention in school. I thought Marshalls was real fancy until my mother took me to Hit Or Miss right before ninth grade. I walked in and couldn't believe it. Now THAT was nice. It wasn't all jumbled up and messy like Marshalls, and it didn't sell housewares and have a gardening section like Kmart. It was the first time I went to a grown-up place for school clothes.

My mother bought me a pink, white, and gray knit V-neck sweater vest. It. Was. Perfect. I put it in my closet with such care and pride you'd have thought it was a Pulitzer Prize. It was to be the centerpiece of my ninth-grade wardrobe. I

couldn't wait until the first day of school to wear that fucking vest. I LOVED it and I remember everyone, teachers included, admiring it and asking where I'd gotten it. I was so
so cute in my vest and my new jeans with the CREASE in them.
Oh man. Remember when a crease in a new pair of jeans was
the LOOK?! Nowadays if you spy someone with creased pants
you'd be, like, *Look at this herb.* But back then it meant they
were new and you were stylin'.

It was important to my mother that we looked presentable
and she led by example. Deborah Sirleaf is what one might
call "chichi" and looks very much a diva. You'd never know
we had modest means by her fabulous attire, most of which
she made herself. If she's to attend an event she is no doubt
making her dress because, as she put it in her ever-present
Liberian accent, "Whhhat? I wooden be caught deeeead in
dih sim dress as someone else. What? Not me-oh." She is always "dressed." We may have been poor but my mom always
looked regal. She's a champion of the monochromatic look—
top, skirt, shoe, purse, headband—all the same color. She loves
shoulder pads, manicured nails, and as much jewelry as one
can possibly wear. Her signature look these days is the sheer
shirt with matching bra underneath and maxi-skirt. People
wear bathing suits under cover-ups that are see-through all
the time, but when it's your mom, it's like, okay, can we cover
it up a bit? There isn't a body of water in sight and Mom
looks like she's poolside at Club Med.

In high school I'd get so embarrassed because I thought
she was a lil' sexier than a mom should be. If she had to pick
me up from a practice at the school I'd ask her not to get out
of the car. "Please don't come with me to school!" Mom wore

those wide-width corduroy leggings (which she called bub-blegum leggings, I don't know why) before they were cool. I'd be like, "Why are your pants so tight?"

"Just because you don't have any fashion sense . . ." she'd snap back. "People are always saying how nice I look. They're like, 'Ooooh Debbie! Look at you.'"

My mom be feelin' herself. And I gotta admit, folks be feelin' her, too. I'll never forget when she came to stay with me at college when I had knee surgery. We were at a campus convenience store shopping when one of the football players came over to me. He leaned in all conspiratorially and asked, "Wassup with the new prospect?" as he gestured toward my mom, who was picking out cereal, no doubt looking for the cheapest brand.

I was like, "Prospect? That's not a prospective student. That's my M O T H E R. Back away from me, ya freak." I couldn't believe he was tryna push up on my mom. When I told her she shrugged it off and said, "He's not the first. He won't be the last." LOLOLOLOLOLOL. Aaaahhhhh, Debbie's got jokes.

I was completely unaware we didn't have money until around sophomore year in high school when I started seeing with my own eyes what I was missing out on. My mom got a side job cleaning houses to make extra money and she'd bring me and George with her to help. One time, around Christmas, this family who we cleaned for left all their presents under their real tree in the opened boxes, almost presenting them. Not to make us feel bad; I don't think they were show-ing off or anything like that. I think it was just a tradition of theirs to leave the gifts under the tree. I thought it looked beautifully festive. I remember there were new Reeboks, books, board games, and Champion sweatshirts all on display. Nowadays you can get Champion at Sears, but back then it was an enviable brand. I'll never forget they even had those Beverly Hills Polo Club towels. All I could think was, *Daaaamn these kids cleaned up! Wow. Polo towels from Beverly Hills. Ain't that something?* How extravagant. I mean, who wants to ruin towels from Beverly Hills? If we had towels from Beverly Hills I wouldn't use them.* It looked as though they had had the perfect Christmas. The perfect house—though when I think about it now, they could have updated the decor a little, know what I'm sayin'? But to me at that time, they were living the perfect life.

I couldn't unsee what I saw. I couldn't go back to not knowing we didn't have the things other people had. In high school, my French club went on a class trip to Paris but I didn't even ask my parents if I could go because I just knew I'd get the standard "We're broke. Money is tight." My father, who was measured and quiet and kind, sort of like Droopy Dog but less sleepy looking, found out about the trip after it happened and was upset.

"Why didn't you ask me?"

"Cuz you're always broke, there's no way you could have paid for me to go."

"I would have found a way," he said sadly. He was beat up that I missed out on a trip that I didn't even bother trying to go on. He loves to travel. He values the experience maybe

---

* Years later I found some Beverly Hills Polo Club towels at a Ross and bought one straightaway. Not a set, but *one*. I felt fancy.

more than anything. Now, with his kids out of college and in his retirement, he travels as much as he can. Bottom line, back *then* we couldn't afford it.

I grew to resent my parents' "broke" line. I couldn't wrap my head around how two people with full-time jobs never had money. It just didn't make sense. You get paid every single week, there's no way you're broke. I didn't "get" what bills were. I didn't know the value of a dollar. I didn't know jack shit about money. I just knew I didn't like being left out and I felt entitled to the same stuff my friends had. There was a group who would hit up McDonald's after school, and I never had enough money to buy anything because my allowance was next to nothing. So, one day, when I was about fifteen, when my parents weren't home, I stole money out of this locked jar that my dad would put quarters in every day so I could buy a cheeseburger, fries, and an apple pie. It felt good to be able to participate. That's all I wanted. To be one of the crowd. So I kept taking quarters, until eventually my dad noticed that his coin stash had stopped growing.

When they found out that I had taken the money from that quarter bank, my mother, whose temper rivaled Tony Soprano's, tore into my bedroom and swore I was on drugs because no child of hers "in their right mind" would steal. And steal from the father who sacrifices everything for his family. I *HAD* to be on drugs. She turned my room UPSIDE DOWN, like an FBI raid on the Bada Bing!, dumping every drawer, pulling EVERYTHING out of my closet, flipping the mattress off the bed. She gave me a well-deserved beatdown then left me to clean it all up. It was insane. I got whupped, my room was fucked, and you *know* I got grounded. But worse was my *father's* reaction. It was the next day and my mother told me my father was in the den and that he wanted to talk to me. He was sitting in his recliner watching soccer. I entered apprehensively, heart racing, and stood next to his chair as he stared at the screen.

"I'm really disappointed," he said quietly. "I'm going to keep giving you your allowance until your confirmation, but after that you're going to have to get a job."

He couldn't look at me. That broke me more than my mother beating the shit out of me. I went to my room and cried and cried and cried. My father was disappointed in me and there was nothing I could do.

So, I got my first paid job* at sixteen. I can't believe it took that long for me to get my first job because in my family, we worked. Two jobs if you had to, to make ends meet. Work work work work work.

I got a gig as a cashier at Nichols Discount City, a not-as-cool Target in the dirty Jerz. My father wouldn't let me work in fast food; after all, it was my neeeed for fast food that landed me in this predicament in the first place. I also think he was scared I'd spend all my earnings on cheeseburgers and fries and apple pies. I hustled my ass off at Nichols and was such a good employee I was promoted after three months to train all the new kids on the register. Wasn't long† before I found out that a boy I trained was making more money than me. And a girl. She made less than him but more than me. (It was all

---

* I *did* help my mom clean houses. I did *not* get paid for it. It was just something I had to do.

† And by "wasn't long" it was literally like two weeks. If *that*.

chump change because I was only making minimum wage at the time but it was the principle.) They were both white. This incongruity was not lost on me and I went directly to the manager.

"I trained Scott and he makes $1.25 more than I do."

"How do you know how much he makes?"

"He told me!"

"You guys shouldn't be discussing how much you make."

"Well, we did and I know. I'm the only black girl on the floor and I trained the two other people there, I'm better than all of them, trust me when I say I don't want to make it weird for you, but it definitely seems like a race thing."

They back-paid me the difference, and then my dad said I could quit because he was so furious. I promptly gave my two-weeks notice and when it was up I walked out of there with my head held high and my pocket full of mad cash for someone who'd never had a job before and was leaving it after six months. It was a great Christmas for my family and me. I made it rain with prezzies.

That was the first time I got a taste of how fucking good it feels to make your own money, and more important, SPEND IT. I put in the work and I wanted to reward myself for my efforts. That's kind of been my financial philosophy ever since. This was very different from my father the saver. I'm not the type to stash ALL my cash away for a rainy day. Probably because I didn't have three kids, four nieces, a cousin-in-law (that's eight dependents), and a mortgage like my dad did. I was without obligations. I was earning my own money and was going to enjoy it, with some limits. But first I was about to learn those limits.

I was one of those suckers in college who signed up for a "starter" credit card with a crazy-high interest rate at the campus bookstore and then immediately bought shit I couldn't afford.

Duke sweatshirts.

Duke sweatpants.

Duke messenger bag.

Duke pajamas.

Did I mention I went to Duke? Go Devils!

I'd get a bill and think nothing of it. Seriously, I thought N O T H I N G of it. When you get a bill you normally think, *At some point, I'm going to have to pay this bill.* Not me. That minimum payment and due date were merely suggestions that I could or could not adhere to.

There were definitely times when my $500-limit card was declined but because it happened to so many of us freshman suckers, it wasn't even embarrassing. Today if my card gets declined, something is undoubtedly wrong on the creditor's end, and I'm making indignant calls cuz my shit stayyyys correct. But back then I didn't even know that I should be humiliated. You live and you learn, right? If I'm at a restaurant and see a waiter giving someone the "bend-down whisper" I immediately get uncomfortable for them.

I eventually took my credit very seriously. I think anyone with shitty credit who tries to buy a house for the first time has a moment where they think, *Oh, THAT's what they were talking about when they said you need good credit.* I learned that shit the hard way. My credit score was shite by the time I finished college and even worse by the time I moved to LA.

I took great pains to fix my credit rating* and am almost as proud of that as I am of getting my degree. I'll never forget the first time I got a letter notifying me that my credit card limit was being increased without me requesting it. Say word? You wanna give me $9,000 to spend? Holy shit! I hit the mother lode! What *shall* I buy? My shit is so legit these days I'm up to $35,000.† I could buy a boat on that card! It'd be one of those cheap-ass dinghies they give away in the Show-case Showdown on *The Price is Right* but it still qualifies as a sea vessel.

I wouldn't say I'm quote unquote *good* with money, but I'm not irresponsible. I'm not rich. I'm what you'd call "comfort-able." I'm in a place now where I make enough money that I can get what I want when I want it, not miss my mortgage payment, help my parents, pay my reps their 10 percent, and still have money in the bank. I don't want a Rolls-Royce. I don't need a jet. I don't need a place in the Alps. Those aren't the things I want. I want to go out for dinner and I want to go on vacation. I don't need a giant mansion. I'd be cool with a McMansion. It'd have to be a manageable enough size that I could afford to pay someone to keep it clean. I do, *however*, want a claw-foot tub. Scratch that. I like the look of a clawfoot tub but I don't want to fuck around with getting in and out of one. No sense in bustin' my ass when all I want is a good soak.

---

* I could run a short seminar on how to fix your credit score. I had to do a lot of work in order to get my mortgage loan but the hustle paid off. Perhaps I'll put out a pamphlet.

† I KNOW there are higher limits to be had, but for me this shit is BANANAS. It's no AmEx black card, but it makes me feel helluh baller.

I'd prefer a sunken oversize Jacuzzi tub that I can easily step into. I saw in a magazine once that they make double-paned glass walls with crystals inside so that when you flip a switch the crystals rotate and the glass becomes opaque. You can have all the natural light you want during the day but you can bathe in privacy with the flip of a switch. If that ain't some baller shit I don't know what is. *THAT's* the shit I want.

And I want an elevator. I don't like stairs. I got two bum knees and a raggedy right ankle. An elevator would do nicely in my next crib. One of my *Parks and Rec* costars has a gorgeous house in Bel Air that has an elevator and a hot tub that can accommodate a medium-size dinner party. The whole back of his house is glass, and if the lights are on, the neighbors can see all ya business. I probably should've mentioned to him the existence of rotating crystal walls but I'm keeping that amenity for *my* dream house.

Now that I'm working in TV, I make more money than my parents did and live a different life. That's my new normal. And that's what parents want for their kids, right? We made the best of our situation growing up and now I'm doing the same, just with a little more money in the bank. But I haven't forgotten where I come from. Growing up on the dodgy side of middle class is a part of me. It's who I am at the core. To this day, I cut open lotion tubes and I use soap until the bar completely disappears into my washcloth. And it was a long time before I gave myself permission to have nice things because NICE = EXPENSIVE. And expensive was out of reach. As I got older, I started to make my own rules. I decided that since I earn my own money, I can allow myself a few niceties.

People may think because someone is on TV they've got

money to burn like sage in a haunted house. Not true. I have to act like I have SOME sense. I do like a bargain and can do some real damage in Target. I have been known to set my alarm for 7 a.m. to log on for a sale on HauteLook.com. I hoard frequent-flier miles and I WILL charge Funyuns to my American Airlines MasterCard at the gas station so I get my points.

I don't fear being poor again. I don't think I'd fall back to living in the projects, knock on wood. I don't think I'll ever have to eat ramen with American cheese again, unless I choose to. But even if I don't make as much money in the future, I have my family and my friends, my flat screen, my Netflix, and my membership to Amazon Prime. They make me happy. They bring the joy. The *things* in your life don't have to be expensive for you to thoroughly enjoy them.

Don't get me wrong, I enjoy money. I like making it and I like spending it. I just don't *need* to be obscenely rich. But if my friends ask me to go on a vacation to Hawaii, I want to be able to go. And, fuck it, I want to fly first class. I've worked hard and gotten paid shit for a long time and now I actually *can* afford it.

In case you were wondering, THAT is how I treat myself.

Chapter Four

Louis and Gucci and Pucci, Oh My!

I wasn't always the fashion plate the world knows me to be today. Wait, the world *does* think I'm a fashion plate, right? Quick question: What is a fashion *plate*, exactly? Asking for a friend. Anyway, the WORLD may not think I'm fashionable, but enough people have complimented my style that I believe I'm at least moderately sty*lish*. This wasn't always the case. I had a very narrow idea of fashion, if you could call it an idea at all. I was pretty much a plain Jane. I never wore jeans in college until my junior year.

All my girls strutted around campus in form-fitting Phat Farm or DKNY, but not me. It wasn't because I was an Orthodox Jew or Mormon or Jehovah's Witness and had an imposed dress code. I just wasn't petite. I was and *am* a big girl and I never thought jeans fit me right. It's the same reason, for most of my teens and into my twenties, I didn't like dresses or skirts. The muumuu look wasn't my jam and so I preferred a uniform of slacks with button-down shirts or flow-y tops. I had convinced myself that this look was cute. In fact, the slacks-button-down look was such a part of my style that on my first red carpet I ever walked for *Parks and Rec*, I wore white pants and a pink Polo shirt, size 4X, the better to hide my body, or so I thought. I now realize that those huge shirts made me look even bigger than I was. Talk about counterproductive.

So what changed to turn me into the diva of swagu? A few years ago, a friend dragged me to a Dressbarn and forced me to try on dresses. Okay, she didn't *force* me. I mean no one forces a diva to do anything she doesn't want to. I hadn't worn a dress in ages, had recently lost a few pounds, and thought perhaps I should try this dress thing as my slacks-button-down red-carpet look could use some adjusting. And you know what? I was pleasantly surprised at how cute ya girl was lookin'. I found a mod A-line swing dress that hugged my curves where I wanted it to hug me. I couldn't believe it. That shit fit! It was an emotional moment looking at myself in the mirror, loving the way my body looked in a dress I chose because I liked it and not because it hid me. I looked like I had a shape! A shape other than that of a cube. Because I have boobs that are bigger than my waist in a dress that hugged me on top, I looked shapely! Yassss, queen.

I looked good and I liked it. After discovering Dressbarn, I fucking went nuts. I finally got a taste of what many women experience when shopping, that adrenaline rush that comes with getting something perfect and new and I wanted more more MORE. Unfortunately, it quickly became clear that I'd gotten lucky at Dressbarn and the search for other stylish dresses in my size would be like trying to find a polar bear in a snowstorm. It's possible but you gotta look real fuckin' hard, and nine times out of ten it's gonna be in some obnoxious pattern even Miley Cyrus wouldn't sport.

In the past, I'd only really shopped at Lane Bryant, which had been solid (and still is). I soon discovered Ashley Stewart and I was blown away by how supercheap her stuff was, which is good and bad depending on what you're shopping for. Cute outfit for the friend of a friend's barbecue? Great. Formal dress for the Peabody Awards? Not so much. Other than that, much of what I found was way too expensive (cough cough Marina Rinaldi—I wait for that end-of-season sale and even then I give a lot of side-eye to what the final price is AFTER 30 percent off) and rarely worth it to me (Eileen Fisher, I love your stuff but I can't with your $200 tanks and camis. I just can't). The old reliables quickly became unreliable as the Nordstrom and Bloomingdale's closest to me stopped carrying plus sizes. I have since turned to online sites like ASOS, SimplyBe, and fullbeauty.com, but the struggle continues to be real when it comes to finding sexy, appealing, comfortable, affordable, fashion-forward clothing in my size. It bums me out and also makes me angry and sometimes a little embarrassed that I can't look the way I want to.

To add insult (size 11½ feet, anyone?) to literal injury— I've had two knee surgeries and an ankle surgery—I can't even relish becoming a shoe whore. Because of my unfortunate boat feet and two bad wheels I have to wear completely flat shoes, which has relegated me to sneakers, flip-flops, and a sad array of sandals and comfort flats. Not a sexy heel in the bunch. Not even a chunky platform cuz that's a pratfall waiting to happen and I ain't the one! I tried to get into hats. I own a ton of baseball hats, but that look came to a screeching halt when I went through a Bojangles' drive-through in North Carolina wearing one and the guy kept calling me "Sir." I've got some tig-o-bitties, how are you calling me "Sir?" It made me so mad I stopped wearing baseball hats. I also own a truckload of newsboy caps and fedoras. They're adorable and add an air of mystery to my look but they make me lazy and I feared my hair would eventually become one thick dread-lock. And the last thing I wanna look like is a hippie surfer who dropped out of boarding school and moved to Hawaii to live in his Saab on the beach.

I just wanted to be down with the couture club. But when it came to being a fashion icon, it appeared that I was gon' be shit outta luck. Or was I? There *was* something that could move me into the fashion light. I don't know how it took me so long to realize it but it finally made itself obvious to me. I was vacationing for the first time in Rome and I found my-self in need of *something*. I didn't know what it was, I just knew there was something calling for me. As I strolled near Piazza di Spagna, aka the Spanish Steps, and onto Via dei Condotti and past Gucci, I saw it:

The Designer Handbag.

Handbags! Gorgeous, sophisticated, delightful handbags. Here was some designer shit I could wear! Because hand-bags never don't fit. That was a double negative but it feels right. There are a myriad of bags that "fit" me. Top handles, crossbodies,* baguettes, fold-over clutches, envelope clutches,

---

* It is possible that the crossbody could be ill-fitting if the strap is too short. This can be problematic if you are tall, short, or top-heavy. If the crossbody doesn't fit right I will take it in to be adjusted or order a longer strap. It costs a bit more but is a small price to pay for a bomb-ass bag.

hobos, messengers, satchels, shoppers, totes, wristlets, shoulder bags, saddle bags, barrel bags, doctor bags, bowling bags, duffel bags, you name it. I can wear 'em ALL and buy 'em all. So I do. Good Lord, do I ever.

When I was a kid, I was oblivious to the seduction of a structured handbag, immune to the charms of a classy clutch. Sure, I had that lavender satin snap-top purse that I wore on special occasions, like Christmas or Easter. And I had one bag I loved from Hit Or Miss that had a pretty pastel picture of a 1940s blonde pinup wearing a sailor's cap on it. It looked like a pop-art drawing. I loved it. Otherwise I wasn't that preoccupied with purses.

My mother, on the other hand, had a big collection of purses, even a Gucci bag—which we're pretty sure "fell off a truck"—that she got from a shady uncle, but my bags of choice were more of the tomboy, utilitarian variety—backpacks, messengers, a LeSportsac knockoff, and then there was the olive-green briefcase I carried around in college. I got it from T.J. Maxx and I thought it was kinda fancy. It wasn't. It was plastic and unnecessary. But that's where I was back then.

My friends were rocking that Coach bucket bag and it was a big deal. *Damn, that's niiiiice*, I thought, as I stroked their new, fresh, buttery-leather bags. That's what I wanted—my OWN Coach bag. Nothing was gonna stop me from getting myself that Coach bag. Nothing but that $300 price tag. Say whaaaaaaa? Three hundy? For a muhfuhkin purse? You must be out yo COT DAMN mind!

I was a broke college student; three hundy for a purse wasn't gon' happen. But I was still itchin' to fit in on the handbag front. I needed to find something in my price range. I went to Marshalls on the hunt for something comparable. All I could find to hold me over was a $100 Anne Klein bag that had been marked down from $200. *Ooh, I got me a designer puuuurse!* I thought, all proud.

Markdowns and knockoffs would have to do until I started making real money. I had major purse envy but my time was a-comin'. Once I got my first job out of college at the pharmaceutical firm, my first paycheck was already spoken for. I'll never forget the day I walked into that Coach store, feeling myself. I was about to DO the damn thing. I browsed the pristine shop, admiring how lovely the floor plan was. Everything in its rightful place. This was nothing like Marshalls. Marshalls was like the ruins of a bombed-out city compared to this utopia. The signature bucket bag was no longer in production so I would have to find something else. I eyed several bags but nothing gave me the tingling feeling I had hoped for until I saw it. Just as I was about to give up hope on finding something I spied her. She was hanging on a brushed-iron stand. She was a brown suede floppy bag with a flap and a more-than-ample strap. She was soft, supple, and flawless. She even smelled good. She smelled like a . . . well, she smelled like a Coach store, new and crisp. I caressed the suede gently with the backs of my fingers the way soul mates caress each other in a Nicholas Sparks novel.

"It's soft, huh?" the salesperson whispered to me.

It sure was, and it was MINE. I handed over my debit card to that clerk for the very first—and most definitely not the last—time. Then my beautiful bag was placed inside another bag that said COACH on it, cuz that's how they do it there. They

put your bag in ANOTHER bag.* If that ain't some fancy shit I
don't know what is. I walked out of that store chest puffed
and head high. Had it been a scene in a movie, the song playing would've been Drake's "Fancy."

My purse obsession was officially on like Donkey Kong.
It was also the beginning of my suede obsession, a phase I
regret because suede is a bitch to keep clean. At first, I only
bought Coach bags because that's all I knew. It wasn't until
yeeeears later that I realized I hadn't even scratched the designer handbag surface until that day on Via dei Condotti in
Rome. Coach was cute but Gucci was elegant. That first Gucci purchase was a simple suede beige bucket bag. It didn't
have the Gucci GG's all over it. Just a small logo on the
handle. I remember my friend Lex saying, "You're buying a
Gucci and it doesn't even say 'Gucci' on it? If I'm gonna pay
for a Gucci bag everybody is gonna know it's a GUCCI BAG!"
Hahahaha. I laugh every time I think of that moment. For
me it wasn't about the label on the outside. Don't get me
wrong, I'm as much of a label whore as the rest of 'em but it's
more internal. I need to *know* that my shit's authentic. It's not
as important to me that EVERYONE know the authenticity of
my bag. It IS, however, important that people who *know* bags
know that my shit is legit. By the way, I got a lot of compliments on that bag and whenever someone would get close
enough for a better look, they saw it was a Gucci and it took
the admiration to the next level. *That* was enough for me.

I love that bag and it will always have a special place in my

---

* Medium to high-end shops place their handbags in what is called a
"dustbag" to protect them. The handbag is to be stored in the dustbag.

heart, but I fell even harder for another brand. If Coach popped my purse cherry and Gucci was the good sex you have once you know how to do it, then Louis Vuitton is that love affair that makes you sick to your stomach when you think about it coming to an end. It's that one lover you can never forget, and her name is Alma.

The Louis Vuitton Alma PM in vernis is an iconic classic that has been around since the 1930s and has an embossed patent-leather monogram. I own four of those puppies, in ivory, black, light blue, and military green, and I'm so ABOUT them. I've even given them names like they're pets. Pearl, Midnight, Skye, and The Major. Hey, don't judge. Some people name their vibrators, I name my purses!

With every new purse came a greater interest in designer bags. Lucky for me my career advancement coincided with my need to add to my collection. I started following Instagram accounts that showcased designer bags. One in particular, @upcloseandstylish, keeps me salivating.

My tastes change the more I follow trends and pay attention to what's hot and what's not. I no longer like the bucket shape. It's chaos in those bags. They're like black holes. Nothing sends an uncomfortable shiver through me like watching someone root around in the bottom of a bucket bag looking for their keys, only to pull out crumpled dollar bills and a partially unwrapped stick of gum covered in hair. How about you take the hair off the brush before you put it in the purse? I can't stand loose hair floating around in a purse. And bucket bags are notorious for debris. I now prefer a structured bag in which I can place a purse organizer with ample compartments for all my essentials. They are neat and can be moved from purse to purse with ease. As a person who likes to change up her purse as often as I change underwear, a purse organizer is a gift from on high because switching purses is just tedious.

Is my bag obsession compulsive? Perhaps. Like Lay's potato chips, I can't have just one. While we're checking off psychological deficiencies, I guess I'm a tiny bit impulsive, too. I've been known to stroll into Nordstrom and walk out minutes later with a jaguar-print Gucci stirrup bag and matching scarf, neither of which was exactly within my budget but the print was very on trend. What's a gal to do? My theory, my motto, the words I live by, is this: If you see something in the store, and you think it's too expensive so you walk away but you find yourself still thinking about it, go back and get it. Nothing will break your heart like dawdling about because you think something isn't worth the price and then finally deciding you MUST have it and it's no longer available to you. I learned that shit the hard way. I remember seeing a white Chanel Cambon bag on the shoulder of one of the overprivileged kids on MTV's *Laguna Beach: The Real Orange County* and falling truly, madly, deeply in love. I couldn't keep my eyes off of it any time she sported that thing. I convinced myself that I could not afford Chanel. But the bag would not leave my mind until one day I finally went to Chanel on Rodeo Drive and inquired about the bag only to find that it was discontinued. I was sick to my stomach. I never wanted it more than when I knew for sure I could absolutely not have it. I bought a different Chanel that day but I'll never forget the one that got away. That hurts my heart to this day. I have so many outfits that would go perfectly with that bag.

I wasn't going to make that mistake ever again. So, one day while I was showing a friend an army-green Louis Vuitton Alma bag I had been visiting in the shop for a few weeks, the salesgirl noticed my unabashed admiration for its unique beauty. She said hi, mentioned it was an employee favorite, then walked over to the computer, typed some shit and frowned. "That's a seasonal color, it won't be around very long," she warned. Then she hit me with, "There are only two left in North America."

Fuck you, bitch!

Really?

Is that how we're playing this?

Shit.

Sold.

Then you know what that charlatan had the balls to do? She showed me the matching wallet. The fuck?? Ugh. I said, "Put that on there, too, and speak no more words until I leave this establishment."

Look, I'm not about to Chapter 11 myself for a purse but if I have to eat ramen with American cheese for a few months to get me a Gucci, so be it. For example, the holy grail of handbags is the Hermès Birkin bag, a handmade, saddle-stitched masterpiece that comes in a range of exotic skins—calf leather, ostrich, lizard—and it can cost up to $150,000. Hermès limits the supply on purpose to create exclusivity, and it is nearly impossible to get a brand-new one unless you're like the princess of Qatar or Oprah. And now that I think about it, I'm not even sure Oprah has the pull necessary to get first dibs on a new Birkin. Even then, it's like a six-year waiting list. You're more likely to win the Powerball or get struck by lightning or both (I tell you, those lottery winners are all cursed!) before you get a new Birkin bag.

So anyway, one day, after a pretty devastating breakup, I was at a friend's house for a swim workout when I had to use the little girls' room. I got out of the pool, found the loo, pulled down my wet bathing suit with all my strength, sat down on the toilet and started scrolling through my phone. Don't you dare say "ew," you know you do it, too. Suddenly an alert from HauteLook.com popped up in my notifications. I clicked on it. A new, rare, signature orange Birkin was on sale RIGHT NOW for . . . $15,000. My heart started racing and I felt sick. But not sick like I might throw up. Sick like my live-in boyfriend of five years just got on his knees at the restaurant and is holding a black velvet box in his shaky hands.

Five minutes later I walked back out to the pool.

"I'm scared to tell you what I just did," I said to my friend.

"What did you do?" she asked, alarmed, like maybe I'd broken something irreplaceable in the house.

"I just bought this bag."

"What bag?"

"A Birkin bag."

"Seriously? I'm scared to ask. How much?"

"Fifteen."

"Oh, wow, fifteen hundred? For you that's good."

"Fifteen THOUSAND."

"You just spent fifteen grand on the pot??"

"I know. I feel like a Hilton."

It's true, people. I bought a bag on the bowl. Basically, I charged the equivalent of a Honda Civic on my credit card in less than forty seconds. It may have been an impulse buy—retail therapy to nurture my broken heart—but don't they always say to go with your gut? Whoever "they" are. I went into justification mode. It was a BARGAIN! That bag would normally cost *at least* $30,000!

I don't regret what I did. My Birkin is my most prized possession and I take excellent care of it, along with the fifteen Louis, twelve Guccis, and dozens of other bags I've collected over the years. Chanel. Armani. Badgley Mischka. Tom Ford. Bulgari. Saint Laurent, formerly YSL. Red-carpet clutches in an array of colors. Bags for the beach. Bags for festive occasions. Bags for business meetings. Bags for summer. I built special shelves in my closet and installed a spotlight to showcase them like museum pieces. I try to be diligent about cleaning makeup off my hands before handling the more delicate ones because it can be absorbed into the material and there's no getting it out. I'm extra careful when wearing new denim so as not to stain my patent leathers. (P.S. This goes for light-colored leather car seats as well.)

As careful as I am, I enjoy the shit out of my purses and I don't get *too* precious about it all. When it comes down to it, a bag is just a thing. I've got pen marks on my Tory Burch and dripped butter pecan ice cream on my Michael Kors. I've been known to use my feet to get my Louis under the seat in front of me on an airplane, and I even took my Birkin to a Cracker Barrel. Hermès and Cracker Barrel, that's how it was meant to be! I took a pic of my bag right next to my Momma's Pancake Breakfast and posted it on Instagram. Yessir. I sure did.

I used to worry about using my "nice" bags too much and ruining them but what's the point of buying 'em if you're not gonna use 'em? By the time you go to wear them, they're not "in" anymore. You just wasted time. Bitch, you bought it, use it! I've done that with clothes before—saved them for some special occasion that never came. Then when I started wearing my "good" stuff to random shit, people would say, "Why are you so dressed up?" Because I own it and it's clean! You gotta rock it in real time or you're that girl wearing chiffon to the all-you-can-eat brunch buffet.

I'm proud of my purse collection. I don't have expensive clothes or cars or that mansion with a claw-foot bathtub, so this is the way I reward myself for working my ass off. It also makes me feel good about myself. I feel a sense of accomplishment in my professional life and I get to celebrate it in my personal style.

I know what I like and I get them when I want them. I never thought I'd get a Birkin bag and yet there is a Birkin bag in my closet. I'd like to say that I'd never spend more money on a new purse than on a Tesla. But I can't and won't make that promise . . . because I haven't seen that bag yet!

I know that I don't need expensive designer clothes to bring out my inner swagu. You just need items that look good on you and make you feel good. You can be fabulous in clearance-rack gear. As long as you know you're the shit, everyone else will get it, too. And a shiny new Louis V doesn't hurt, either.

And, in case you're wondering, that is ALSO how I treat myself.

Chapter Five

What's Up Doc?

I was in the airport in Chicago a bunch of years ago when I ran into a former classmate from college. We'd both been pre-med though she was two years ahead of me and she was a neurosurgeon now.

"Holy shit. What is up? What are you doing here in Chicago?"

"I have a show tonight at Northwestern," I said.

"A show? What kind of show?"

"Comedy. I do stand-up."

"Shut the hell up. You're a comedian?"

"Yeah. What are you doing here?"

"I was here for a neuroscience conference."

"So, what are you, a brain surgeon?" I asked, a bit sarcastically.

"Yeah," she said matter-of-factly.

I remember feeling a twinge of jealousy. I was hustling and successful among my LA comedy friends, but my friends from college were working as doctors and surgeons. Soooo many of my college peers were successful physicians. A close friend at the time was a radiologist in Georgia. I visited once when I was on tour and couldn't get over her house. They were installing a pool at the time and I kept thinking, "Are they hosting the Olympic trials?" It was enormous.

Now this chick standing in front of me at Hudson News was going to a fancy conference about extracranial cerebro-vascular systems and I was about to go tell a bunch of hung-over students a funny story about how I once went to Kentucky Fried Chicken and they ran out of chicken.*

Why the fuck did I not go to medical school? What was I thinking?

You know that saying, "If you want to make God laugh, make plans?" It's so true that life doesn't always go in the di-rection you think it will. Ever since I can remember, I wanted to be a doctor. From my early days watching Dr. Huxtable on NBC to therealdrmiami on Snapchat today, I've always had an affinity for medicine. I don't know where it came from. It's not like we had doctors in my family. It certainly wasn't our family business. My parents never said I needed to go to college to become a doctor. I just always wanted to be one. I take that back. I always thought I *needed* to be one.

And it's not like I had a particularly high tolerance for blood and guts. All I know is that I always had one goal in mind—get my MD. If it were up to my early childhood edu-cators, though, I'd have never made it. When I was seven, I spent a year in Liberia with my mom, and when I got back, my American elementary school threw me into remedial classes without even testing me. When I was old enough to

---

* The first real bit I ever wrote. One might call it my signature bit. Perhaps I'll share later.

question it, I assumed it was because I was black and had a Liberian accent.

I was so fucking bored in my second-grade classes, I once fell asleep and my teacher didn't bother to wake me up. She and I both knew that I knew two plus two equals four, two times two equals four and two divided by two equals one. It was basic and I needed more of a challenge. Every year I'd jump up a level, and by the time I reached seventh grade, I was in the top classes, the more challenging classes. I had a brain, people, and I wasn't afraid to use it. In fact, I *wanted* to.

Education was beyond important in my house. I assumed it was a Liberian thing, because my American friends didn't seem as pressed to excel in school. I remember one afternoon walking home from the bus stop with a group of my friends. Report cards had come out that day. They were all tallying how much money they were gonna get for their grades. Ten dollars for an A. Five dollars for a B. Two dollars for a C.

I was confused.

"Wait a minute. You get paid for grades? You get paid for *C*'s?"

The *FUCK*? I was expected to get good grades or I was in BIG trouble. As a matter of fact, I used to get all A's but I got many an ass whoopin' due to the "COMMENTS SECTION."

> *Comment: Marietta talks a little too much*
> *in class.* → Ass whoopin'
> *Comment: Marietta is a bit of a social*
> *butterfly.* → Grounded for a week

I need to backtrack for a moment. I said I got all A's. That's not completely true. I think I got two, maybe three B's in my grade school to high school career. But, once, I got a C. Yeah, you guys, a mother f'ing C. It was traumatizing. I'm sure you're dying to know what it was in. You're probably thinking it was in gym. Or maybe sewing. Something you can't really study for. Nope. It was in typing. Ty-ping. Can you believe that shit? I have never been so haunted by a grade as I was by that C in seventh-grade typing. If I were in that class now I still don't know how I'd do because who the F uses a typewriter? I know if I were tested on my texting abilities I'd score through the roof. But it was typing that became my middle school Achilles' heel.

My parents were super serious about school and pretty strict about what extracurricular activities they allowed us to participate in. I wasn't allowed to just hang out whenever I felt like it, like some common street thug. I was supposed to be a good, obedient Christian girl, so I was expected to "act right." Because I was afraid of being told no and feeling as though I'd brought shame on the family, I never asked to do things like go to parties or stay out late post my after-school activities. I mean . . . it wasn't as bad as it sounds. It was kinda like on *Orange Is the New Black*. Yes, they *are* in prison but they're allowed to roam the facility freely. My parents did allow particular extracurriculars—the more I did, the better my chance to get into a good college. So, I was on yearbook committee and student council. I was on the calculus team and in the French club. I managed the wrestling team. I ran winter and fall track and by "ran" I mean I threw shot put, discus, and javelin. I also made the cheerleading squad at Matawan Regional High School, home of the Huskies. I wore the maroon and gray with pride. When it came time for my individual,* I hit 'em with a roundoff and a front handspring into a Flying Dutchman with a crash split. I was *ABOUT* some cheerleading. So much so that I earned the "Spirit Award" my senior year. Not bragging. It is what it is.

I was a really good kid . . . okay, fine, I was a blerd, a black nerd—I played chess, taught Sunday school, attended physics parties, and knew how to write in calligraphy—but I had my ways of rebelling. I'd sneak out of my house to go to the school dances. I'd just put my cheerleading uniform on, tell my parents I had a game, and walk right out the front door with my *dance* outfit hidden in my cheerleading bag. As far as I was concerned, a dance was a rite of passage and as long as I didn't hurt anyone or get hurt I could justify deceiving the parentals.

I never got caught. I did come close one time when I snuck home one night and couldn't get in the back door. I had to throw rocks up to my brother's room and have him come down and unlock it. It was a hair-raising sitch for a Sunday school-teaching mathlete, but what a rush to pull it off! Why? Because my parents didn't spare the rod. In our house you did as you were told and were respectful. I never understood kids who talked back to their parents. Whenever I saw it happen I'd watch with my mouth agape. It was beyond my comprehension. I once got the death stare for sighing too loud

---

* An "individual" in cheerleading is the gymnastic performance you do for the player you're assigned. Ours began with "John Smith, he's my man, if he can't do it no one can!" followed by your sweet moves.

after being told to rewash dishes that I hadn't cleaned properly. My mother looked at me with such fiery disbelief, I thought she might burn a hole through my face like Cyclops in *X-Men: The Last Stand*. I can't envision what would've happened had I let actual words out of my mouth.

So, as you can probably guess, my clandestine escapes were few and far between because (a) I didn't want to get my ass beat and (b) school was super important to me. I was going to get into a good college and become a doctor. No, not just a doctor, a NEUROSURGEON, because neurosurgeons were top docs doing highly sophisticated and complicated procedures. I liked a challenge. A real challenge. Learning the elements on the periodic table was a challenge. Synaptic polarization is challenging. Typing isn't challenging. How DID I GET A *C* IN TYPING???? Such bullshit. Uuuggghhh. I'm sorry. I can't let it go.

I was always a good time. I was funny, the proverbial class clown. But as smart as I *was*, I did something not so smart my junior year. I only applied to one college, my dream school, Duke University. When my mother found out, she about had a stroke. "What if you don't get in? Don't think you're living here," she said with a look that almost made me believe her.

Fuckballs. So I applied to three more schools but it was like the Goldilocks process of elimination: UCLA (too far away), Rutgers (too close to home), and Brown (too bad, the deadline had already passed but my mom insisted I apply anyway, wasting time and the $40 application fee).

By the grace of God and, let's be honest, my bomb-ass GPA . . . I got into Duke University! Hallelujah! I was heading to North Carolina to fulfill my dream of becoming the first physician in Sirleaf family history!

Or was I?

As thrilled as my mother and I were the day I got that large 9 × 12 envelope (as opposed to the small white one—large envelopes meant acceptance, standard-size envelopes meant rejection), the look on her face quickly turned to concern. Duke was expensive and she didn't know if they could pay for it. I would have to wait until my father came home to learn my fate.

I went to my room and immediately started to cry. I knew how this went. "We're broke. Money is tight. We don't have it." I'd been hearing it for years. Add to that the fact that Rutgers was closer, so much cheaper, AND had offered me a ton of money and there was no way I was going to Tobacco Road.

As I sat in my room trying to figure out why EVERYTHING bad happened to *meeee*, I heard my father come home. I could hear my mother's voice downstairs talking to my father but it was like listening to people talk while you're under water. I couldn't make out what she was saying. There was silence for about three minutes and then my father finally responded. I tried desperately to make out what he was saying. It was an eternity before I realized I had been holding my breath. And then I heard my Dad's footsteps go through the kitchen and stop at the stairway. He yelled for me to come down. My heart was beating so hard I could feel it in my eardrums. As I walked down our rickety steps I started to slip into a depression. My life was over and there was nothing I could do.

When I got to the kitchen, my father was standing there still in his Conair work uniform. He said, "I heard you got into Duke. I'm proud of you. It's an expensive school." I felt the tears start to burn in my eyes. Then he said, "We'll figure it out."

I don't know if I'd ever felt more relief in my life. It was like a doctor had said the results were back and I was in full remission and then promised my disease would never return. The burning tears of disappointment turned to those of sheer joy and gratitude.

In order to pay for my schooling, my dad—the greatest father to walk the earth—got a second job working the late shift at Stern's department store in Woodbridge Center mall. We filled out my financial aid paperwork and I was on my way to DUKE FUCKING UNIVERSITY.

Before I left for Durham, I had my whole life plan mapped out and it culminated with the letters MD at the end of my name. But the minute I stepped foot on campus, that all got tossed out the window. Suddenly I had so much freedom. Too much freedom! There really should be a mandatory college course on how to manage one's time and NOT spend all of it eating and watching *Jeopardy* in your new best friend's dorm commons. I could do whatever I wanted, whenever I wanted. So I did. I ate Pepperidge Farm Chessmen and drank Welch's Grape Soda. EVERY. SINGLE. DAY. I played library tag and spent hours discussing the cute boys pledging.

Everything I thought I was going to be—who I was going to be—started to change in college. Starting with my name. I'd been Marietta (Mare-ee-yetta) my whole life,* but in col-

---

* Actually I grew up with my family calling me "Neak." It was a nickname my uncle Memmeh had started. He would literally bounce me on his knee, singing "Neak-o-neak, neak-o-neak." And I would

lege some people would pronounce it MayRetta, the way they pronounced the name of the city in Georgia. Then one evening I hooked up with a guy on our football team and, while getting our mack on, he called me Retta. I was thrown by it and mildly annoyed, but that was not the time to set him straight. I later told my friends how annoyed I was by it so they immediately started calling me Retta. You know how friends do (insert mad side-eye here).

As much as it annoyed me, my new name was kind of liberating. Marietta was the sheltered high school girl who was very responsible, predictable, and organized. Retta liked to let loose a little more, though, make no mistake, Retta was not loose literally. I remained a woman of *healthy* repute. I never had sex in college—hookups only—so I didn't have my sexual awakening during this time. My awakening in college was that I could be an independent person. College was the first time I thought about myself because I was *by* myself. That meant not making my bed if I didn't want to (still wanted to and *did*). Eating pizza at 2 a.m. Studying a little bit less, going to parties a little bit more (still not drinking). It wasn't a big deal that I barely drank back then but if you told me now I could never have a drink again I'd throw you off a building.

I didn't have to drink to have fun. For me, having a good time was becoming a rabid Blue Devil basketball fan. I attended Duke during the school's most historic athletic era—when Grant Hill, Christian Laettner, and coach Mike Krzyzewski led the Blue Devils to back-to-back national championships.

---

laaaauuuugh and laaaauuuugh. And eventually my family started calling me Neak.

I only missed one home game in four years and that was to go to church. It was the only time I attended service while in college because Cameron Indoor Stadium became my church. My mother would NOT appreciate this statement. It's just hyperbole, Mom. I didn't REALLY think Cameron Indoor was my church.

I felt very connected to my fellow fanatics, who worshipped (again, Mom, hyperbole) our team with a fiery passion unlike anything I'd ever seen before. I loved the crazy energy and my classmates' brilliant sense of humor. For example, one ref's name was Richard and whenever he made a bad call, they'd chant, "You suck, Dick!" So rude, but so punny! ← See that? Puns on puns on puns. If we were losing to a team, we'd cheer, "That's alright, that's okay, we will sign your checks one day!" But my favorite moment was when "overweight" Georgia Tech star Dennis Scott, who reportedly almost "ate himself out of basketball," came back from summer break thirty pounds lighter. When his name was announced before the game, the crowd threw an assortment of Hostess snacks onto the court. Rude but satisfying. It took the janitors five minutes to clean it up and our team got a technical foul as a result. Not what we were hoping for but soooo worth it.

One of my proudest accomplishments during college wasn't the A I got on a bio final exam, it was during freshman year when I started a cheer at the football games. I was sitting in the black section. Okay, let me backtrack a bit. At football games the black students would sit in the middle section, close to the sideline. We were only 6 percent of an undergraduate population of six thousand, so we didn't take up much space. I'm not sure if we sat there to cheer along with the cheerleaders or do the Cabbage Patch while next to the band, which was directly to our right, but that's where black folks sat. Who was I to question tradition? Now, it wasn't officially designated the black section but that's what we, the black students, called it. Aaaaaaaanyway, during one of the games, after we made an unexpected touchdown, I started doing this cheer. It was simple, direct, and catchy! It went exactly like this:

"DUKE-DUKE MOTHERFUCKUUHHHHHHHH! DUKE-DUKE!"

After a while I would say the "Duke-Duke motherfucker" part and my friends and others around us would finish with "Duke-Duke!" I did that for four years of football games. A couple of years ago a friend of mine went back for the Duke/Carolina basketball game. While in Cameron, he sent me a text that said, *Yo they still doin' your cheer doe. Duke Duke muh-fuhkuh Duke Duke!* It brought a smile to my face. I couldn't be more honored. #Legacy

So, yeah, Duke was pretty much white while I was there. Ironically, I always say, "I got blacker at Duke." That was probably the biggest transformation I made in college. In high school, a majority of my friends were white and about half of them were Jewish. They say ignorance is bliss. And I was living in bliss because I didn't know that blacks and Jews had had mad drama through the years and tense if not tenuous relations. All I knew was I loved my Jewish homies and wanted in on Hanukkah and eight days of presents. My mother was clueless, too; she loved Jewish people. She would say if anyone could empathize with the struggle of black people, it's Jewish people.

In college, the opposite was true. Most of my friends were black and had had more life experiences around other black people. Because we were such a small group, we gravitated to each other and banded together. It was fun and I learned more about my culture than I ever had. My friends weren't militant but Afrocentric/black hippie types or bourgie Jack and Jill types.* I didn't even know what Jack and Jill was. I became tight with an eclectic group of girls, what you kids might call "a squad" these days, and our sisterhood was everything to me. We would spend hours in one another's dorm rooms and dining halls, laughing, sharing, clowning, and crying. Even rapping. Yes. Rapping. We made up our own raps. Basic. Ass. Raps:

> CRUSTY
> *It's your D-Day*
> *We gotta let you know*
> *We don't wanna bust*
> *but it's only a show*
> *You're* CRUSTY
> *(beat box)*
> *and* ASHY
> *(beat box)*
> *Your hair's growin' in*
> *It's getting real nappy*
> *You* NEED *a perm*
> *And you better make it snappy*
> *It's* ROUGH
> *(beat box)*

---

* Jack and Jill of America is to black folks what debutante cotillion clubs are to white people. At least that's what I liken it to.

and TOUGH
(beat box)
Your regrowth's thick
You can't hide that
You try to play it off
By wearin' a hat
It's COARSE
(beat box)
and HARD
(beat box)
We know we're jonin' hard
We know it's not fair
But your knees really need
Vaseline Intensive Care
They're DRY
(beat box)
Like the DESERT
(beat box)
Your legs are scaly
They need some lotion
You'll find less scales
On tuna in the ocean
They're PARCHED
(beat box)
and CRACKED
(beat box)
We're coming to the end
We know you're all sad
But one more thing
YOUR BREATH SMELLS BAD!

Like I said, basic. But it brought us endless entertainment.

And I didn't JUST do raps with my girls. I sang in the Modern Black Mass Choir. There was a point where I thought I might major in drama, so I took drama classes and was a member of Karamu, the African American theater group. I appeared in *A Day of Absence* and *The Colored Museum* and felt so much pride when I received rave reviews.

Yes, I was pre-med, but I was also broadening my horizons with the arts and my relationships. I was being culturally fulfilled at this predominantly white school. My friends and I went to Black Student Alliance events and to off-campus parties thrown by black fraternities at neighboring universities. And it was weird because whenever we were away from school, we didn't tell anyone we went to Duke. You would kind of feel from black people in Durham a little bit of a vibe of, *You must think you're better than us.* We didn't want people to look down on us for going to a good school. Even when we visited other campuses we wouldn't offer up our Duke credentials. We didn't want to hear "Oh, so you must be smart," because they said it in a way that made you feel like they meant "You must be an asshole."

I've since gotten over it. Now when someone hits me with a venom-filled "You must be smart," I counter with a "Yeah, you mad?" And most of the time it's because they:

a. Couldn't get into Duke.
b. Never even went to college.
c. Went to a school that got their ass beat by our basketball team. I'm looking at you, University of Kentucky.

On campus we experienced racist shit from time to time, but that's not special to Duke. That's everywhere. We got involved with the Black on White Student Symposium after one of my girlfriends was called "nigger" on a bus by a white boy. Another time, at a SigEp party, we overheard a white girl asking a frat brother, "What's up with all the black chicks?" We didn't get mad about it, we just got even. We were that girl's fucking nightmare for the rest of the semester. We dubbed her Monchichi because she had a really small head and every time we saw her at a party or in the library or dining hall, we'd loudly say shit like, "Sure are a lot of black chicks here." "Who let all these black chicks in?!" And then we'd sing the song from the commercial, "Monchichi Monchichi. Oh so soft and cuddly. Put the thumb in the mouth she's really sweet. Fun to wiggle his little feet. Ya ya ya! Ya ya ya! Happy happy Monchichiiiiiiii! I love you Monchichi." She must've thought we were insane. But it made us laugh, and her uncomfortable, and that's all that mattered.

I admit it. We could be bitches. But only if someone put us in the position to warrant our bitchdom. *Some* of us were more easily provoked than others but if one was in it, we were all in it. We could be intimidating, no doubt, always had beef with this one or that group. I, who was a parent's gift on earth, found myself in the middle of the great basketball vs. track team controversy. It started when one of the girls on the basketball team appeared one day with a black eye. When she was asked by her teammates who hit her she said it was a black girl on the track team. She wasn't sure who because it was "dark" so she "couldn't really tell."

From what I remember of the rumors going around, it was her boyfriend who had hit her but she was too embarrassed, so she blamed an anonymous track girl. At least that's what got back to me and, if that was true, she clearly had no idea who was on our track team or she might've made a better choice in incognito assailants. Because, as it turned out, I was one of TWO black girls on our track team and the other one was so fair of skin there was no way she wouldn't have seen her in the dark! (Hahahahaha, this just made me laugh to myself and will have my girlfriends crying.)

Wooooo doggy! Was THAT all the talk on campus. Even some of the players on the men's basketball team were in the mix. Everybody wanted to know how this was gonna go down. It almost came to blows on the patio at a party of one of the guy hoopers. It was dumb and it was insignificant in the grand scheme of things, but at the time it was some Biggie/Tupac shit. That was the end of it on that patio.

It seems more often than not that when we were at a party, there was likely gonna be drama and somebody was prolly gonna get a drink thrown on 'em. I was always mortified when shit devolved into drink throwing but they were my friends, so I couldn't not have their backs. I was guilty by association. And I was cool widdit.

Fine. I can't lie. I used to get into it, too. Having close friends and a support system gave me confidence. Other than my weight, my major insecurity at the time, I felt I could handle some shit. My junior year, I got into a fight with this guy, we'll call him Chad, about . . . I don't even remember what it was about. I followed him up the quad, yelling at him about God knows what as a crowd started to grow around us. I got all in his face. I was a legit crazy person. My friends told me at one point I just kept yelling, "Do you know who I am?! Do you know who I *AM*?!"

He didn't, and guess what, neither did I, really. I came to Duke expecting to become a neurosurgeon but book learnin' was obviously not my priority. I did okay in college but nowhere near as well as I did in high school. I was too serious about having fun. Don't get me wrong. I did the work. My notebooks were works of chemical-reaction art. I was obsessed with those multicolored pens and would redo my notes over and over until they were aesthetically pleasing to my eye. Not only was it pretty, it helped my memorization.

I graduated having fulfilled my pre-med requirements. I was equipped to move on to the next level, and had every intention of doing so, but the more time I spent at Duke finding myself, the more something in the back of my mind reminded me there were other things to find.

After graduation, instead of going directly to medical school, I took a year off to work at the pharmaceutical company GlaxoSmithKline. I was looking to give myself a break from school while I prepared for the MCAT. However, I was afraid to step too far away from the sciences so I got a job doing chemistry for Glaxo. It made sense. Do chemistry during the day, study chemistry at night. It was like getting paid to take an MCAT prep course! Only I didn't study at night. After college I experienced an even greater sense of freedom. I had money to spend and I didn't have to do homework. And since I wasn't doing homework (or studying for the MCAT) I spent a great deal of time watching television. I always say as a latchkey kid that television was my babysitter and now it became the best roommate a gal could have. It kept me company, entertained me when I was bored, and lulled me to sleep when it was time for bed. It also didn't eat my Frosted Flakes and leave hair in the drain, and that alone is grounds for Roommate of the Year.

I got very close to my TV. I would talk to the people on it as if they could hear me. I watched a great deal of stand-up comedy, and sitcoms were my favorite. There came a point where I thought I wouldn't mind doing a sitcom. I'm funny and it would be helluh cool to be a TV star. And thus the seed was planted. I was going to be a TV star and I wanted my own sitcom. I noticed that in a lot of sitcoms the lead was a stand-up comedian:

Home Improvement

Everybody Loves Raymond

Roseanne

The Drew Carey Show

Mad About You

Martin

Logic told me, Be a doctor. My heart told me, Do stand-up . . . get your own sitcom. And so I was going to do stand-up. I found out that the comedy club, Charlie Goodnights in Raleigh, North Carolina, had an open mic. All I had to do was write some jokes, go to Goodnights, tell the jokes, and a sitcom would fall into my lap. Easy-peasy. I decided to write down silly stories about my friends and their pets. I was methodical in my writing. I wrote down where to pause, when to laugh to myself, when to lean on the mic stand and when to raise my right eyebrow to indicate how "ridiculous" the world was. I was a maniac. But you know what? That shit worked! I did a five-minute set to a packed house of mostly NC State students and I killed. It felt good. I was on my way!

The host that night was a road comic named Dan French. He approached me after my set and said he thought I was funny and that I should take his comedy class. He said I'd learn how to write and that he wasn't gonna charge me. This guy was gonna help me become a sitcom star? For free? Hell yeah, playa. Let's do dis.

I took Dan's class and started my life in comedy. I did more open mics and eventually started hosting shows around The Triangle, the area between Raleigh, Durham, and Chapel Hill. Dan gave me gigs here and there to be his middle act. The more I did stand-up, the closer I was to becoming a sitcom star and the further I was from becoming a neurosurgeon. I never took the MCAT. I never went to medical school. After a year of doing peptide chemistry during the day and writing and performing comedy at night, I made the plan to move to LA.

I called my parents to tell them my comedy-star plans. They were surprisingly supportive for people who grounded me for being a social butterfly in school. My mother said, "Really? That's what you want to do? Well, if you're going to do it, do it. Don't half-ass it." I couldn't believe my mom said "ass." She added, "You're carrying around your father's last name so don't embarrass him." Then she put my father on the phone so I could give him the news. I'll never forget my dad's response.

"Whatever you do, just get health insurance. If something happens, your mother and I can't afford to take care of you. What if you get paralyzed?"

Okay! Good talk, Dad.

So that is how I went from being Marietta, future brain surgeon, to TV's Retta. I don't regret any bit of it. I wouldn't change my experience at Duke for anything. It gave me some of my forever friends and provided me with my first taste of independence. But, most important, it taught me to ask myself what I wanted and figure out how to get it. So when I ran into that neurosurgeon friend at Chicago's O'Hare, jealousy was born out of anxiousness. I was anxious to get where I was going, to become a TV sitcom star—not to get to that Northwestern comedy show—and jealous that she had already reached her surgical destination.

I haven't gotten my sitcom . . . yet. But I'm no longer jealous of my peers who are all MD'd up. If for no other reason than I don't need malpractice insurance. One less headache for my dad.

Chapter Six

You Do?
I Don't

Weddings can be emotional, honest, beautiful displays of a couple's love and commitment to each other. They can allow you to bear witness to what true love between two people can be. I still don't want to be a part of your life-changing event because it stresses me out because you're crazy. I don't care who you are, if you're getting married you're going to be a crazy person. Weddings make brides crazy, so, I'm sorry, I love you, but You. Are. Kuh-Ray-Zee. And that is why I absolutely do not want to participate in your wedding. Kill me first. It's best if you just send me a link to your bridal registry and let's call it a day.

That said, it isn't that easy to get out of. I want to relay a story, and tell me if I was in the wrong (I was not). A friend from college called and asked me if I'd be in her wedding. If you're anything like me, this is a "hell no" moment. Lazy people don't like to plan shit. I don't want to help plan your wedding, a bachelorette party, a bridal shower, and I damn sure don't want to plan on being available for your fittings. But she happened to ask me right after I made a New Year's resolution to be less of a hater. I said, "I'll do it, on one condition: I cannot wear a sleeveless, strapless, or spaghetti-strap dress. I have fat arms and I'm immoderately self-conscious about them and I will not wear a sleeveless, strapless, or spaghetti-strap dress."

Her first response was, "Are you serious?"

Yeah, bitch. Undoubtedly.

"Okay, fine, whatever, that's cool."

So then I was like, "I guess it'd be an honor to stand in your freakin' wedding."

A week later, I followed up with an email reiterating that under no circumstance would I wear sleeveless, strapless, or spaghetti-strap dresses. She replied electronically, "LOL I got it, Petey Repeaty!"

So I was like, *Cool*, as I rolled my eyes.

Over the next few weeks, I had some phone conversations with the other bridesmaids who we went to college with and waxed nostalgic about our days of yore at university. We discussed what we should do and how much fun we were going to have in Atlanta that whole week leading up to the wedding. We also marveled at the fact that she was even getting married because her fiancé, with whom we'd also attended college, is gaaaaaaaaaaay.

If you're a fan of *Sex and the City* you probably remember season 5, episode 8, where Nathan Lane plays Bobby Fine and he marries Bitsy von Muffling. The episode is called "I Love a Charade." Yeah, he's that kind of gaaaaaaaaaaay. I wanted to tell my friend's fiancé, "Get out the shaving cream, John, because you've got a beard and its name is Nicole." But, whatever, because at this point I was actually looking forward to hangin' with my girls.

About a month after that, I received from the bride-to-be,

via the internet, photos of the bridesmaid dress options. She'd cc'd all of the bridesmaids and wanted us to vote on our favorite. As in any democracy, majority ruled. In this email were four dresses:

One sleeveless.

One strapless.

TWO with spaghetti straps.

My question to you is this: Was this chick looking to end this friendship? Because if I backed out now then I'm the bitch who bailed on her girl's wedding when, in fact, she was a manipulating trick who just backed me into a corner. Am I right?

Needless to say, I sucked it up because if I didn't, I knew she would talk shit about me and then I'd have to cut her. And even though I know I'd be in the right, slicing a bitch cuz she pulled the okey doke on you is still punishable by law.

So the night before the wedding, at the bachelorette party, which I would not and DID not plan, I found out a bit of gossip. Turns out both of the groom's parents were recovering alcoholics, so the reception was going to be dry.

What?!?!

Look, I'm a drinker. I likes to take it to the head and get ripped up. Now I'm not proud of this, it's not coming from a place of pride, I'm stating a fact. A fact with which this hoodwinking con artist is familiar because junior year, during homecoming, we ended up in the infirmary from alcohol poisoning *together*. So I approached this trick. And she knew somethin' was up 'cause she stepped back and took a defensive position. I looked her in the eye and I said:

"There ain't gon be no liquor at the reception?"

She was like, "Oh no, John's parents don't drink."

"What the hell's that got to do with me?"

"Well, we didn't want them to be uncomfortable."

"Again, what does that have to do *avec moi*? Cuz I can handle my liquor."

But let us recap:

1. You coerced me into participating in this fakakta wedding. (Because he's gaaaaaaaaaaay.)

2. You forced me to expose my fat arms to my fellow alums (three of whom are eligible bachelors whose names now include the tags "Esquire" and "MD") in some eggplant monstrosity, which, by the way, is not a good look for a girl my size. At my first fitting there was a four-year-old in the dressing room who kept telling his mother he saw Barney.

3. I spent a week of my life . . . *in July* . . . in GEORGIA, which, on a good day, could double for the Devil's asshole.

4. And now you're telling me I am to be denied the sweet nectar of the gods because once upon a time, Mr. and Mrs. Kirkpatrick let shit get outta hand????

And that's when something happened to me. Some might describe it as a "disconnect," others might say I SNAPPED. I don't exactly recall what I said but I've been told that it was along the lines of:

"It's because of people like you that we're still in Iraq! No one else will tell you, but your wedding dress makes you look like you're four months pregnant! Sophomore year, your fiancé gave Kevin Cavanaugh a hand job in the stacks of Perkins Library!"

Then I flipped a table like a Real Housewife of New Jersey and stormed the fuck out. Initially, I was upset. But then I remembered I wouldn't have to wear that fakakta eggplant dress.

Needless to say, we no longer speak. I hear she's ready to start having kids. I hear he's really not that into it.*

---

* I gotta fess up. It did not go down like this . . . exactly. This story is a mash-up of all the fucked-up weddings I've been to. I'm sorry, but if I wanted to have any friends left in the world, I had to do it like this. I needed to come clean because the last thing I want is to end up across from Oprah being called a fraud and my career over. I LOVE Oprah. I do NOT LOVE weddings. That is a fact.

Chapter Seven

Knock Knock

How many people here have a friend who annoys you so much you don't know why you continue to let them be your friend? I've got this friend who doesn't like animals but has pets.

"Kelly, why do you have animals?"

"Because I get lonely."

Okay. She's got a bird. The bird essentially lives in a cage. She lets him out but he cannot fly because she had his lower wings clipped. Yet she named this bird Freedom. How much "freedom" does this bird have?

She feeds this bird people food. We went shopping once, we were rushing to get home so we went through the drive-through at KFC. We get back to her place and she has the bird on her lap. She always has the bird on her lap and talks baby talk to it.

"Oh, Free Free Free! Oh, Free Free Free!"

Next thing I know, she starts feeding the bird some of her food.

I was like, "Ummmmm, what are you doing?"

"What? I'm feeding my bird."

"You're feeding your bird BIRD. *This has got to be cruelty to animals."*

"Well, my vet says it's okay."

"I don't want to know what you're feeding the damn dog!"

L ike that little story? Oh good, I'm glad you find it amusing, because I must've told it five hundred times. It's the first comedy bit I ever wrote. I could tell it with my eyes closed. I could tell it in my sleep. I could tell it while in a coma, just blinking my eyes in code like that guy in *The Diving Bell and the Butterfly.*

Not long after I moved to LA, I was chosen to be on *The Jenny Jones Show** for an all-female stand-up showcase and it landed me a college agent who specialized in booking campus tours across America. It's the prize every comic wants, to be paid decent money to travel around the country building your brand and a fanbase while working out your material.

For the next two years, I did more than 300 shows. That's the equivalent of a gig about every other day for my fellow mathletes out there. In reality, I'd get booked for three to five shows per week for several weeks in a row at a bunch of colleges clustered in different regions, then come back to LA for a few days to recoup. I was on the road constantly.

At first, for a Jersey Girl who never went anywhere, I thought it was so cool to travel for work. I'd always been

---

* Jenny Jones was a former comedian who had a daytime talk show from '91 to '03. She dedicated two or three shows to giving new comics a chance to be on television.

intrigued and impressed with air travel. It felt fancy and important, bourgie even, to be flying to all these places. I felt a sense of pride when telling friends, "I have to go to North Dakota and *then* South Dakota for work." And they put you up in hotels. I loved hotels! I loved the idea that I never had to make my bed. I was so high on my jet-set life that I wasn't even disgusted by the petri dishes known as hotel comforters. I was like, "This is my house for the day!" I really thought traveling businessmen were livin' the life, just chillin'. They spent their days on airplanes and their nights in Holiday Inns. Who *doesn't* want that life?

I quickly found out who. It was me. *I* didn't want that life. It was some stressful bullshit. Flying all the time is for the birds, literally (exception: Freedom). And it's fucking North Dakota. After you start staying at the Super 8 on the regular, you start to hate hotels, on the regular. Eventually, you start noticing how nasty that comforter actually is, along with the carpet and the shower curtains and the floor around the toilet. Ugh, I just gave myself the heebie-jeebies.

What I was doing wasn't glamorous at all. It was a JOB. But it paid well. For a broke-ass comic, making up to $900 per show was muh-nee. When you're starting out that is straight baller-baller!

My very first gig, at the University of California, Riverside, was a total mindfuck . . . because it was AWESOME. I was scared shitless, I had to do an hour of material—which is an eternity— for the first time, but I was confident that 70 percent of my set was strong. I'd killed with most of it before and indeed I did that night. But I think that might have just been beginner's luck. I wasn't going to be the next Chris Rock overnight. I'd have to pay my dues just like every other neophyte joke slinger.

I was quickly and unceremoniously inducted into the nooners' club. Nooners are shows booked at colleges during lunch in the campus cafeteria and they are a nightmare of clanging dishes, stank cafeteria food, and a cacophony of discussions ranging from the agricultural economics of Thailand to the annual Kappa Sig hall crawl. I remember once when I was at Duke, my friends and I got our trays of chicken fingers and onion rings in the freshman dorm, expecting to sit down and do recon on how we were gonna get to the Omega Psi Phi party over at UNC that weekend. Instead, the lights went down and this nerdy Jewish guy with his shirt tucked into his jeans <<gag>> stood on a makeshift stage and started telling corny jokes about his laundry and in particular his socks. We were like, "The fuck is this bullshit?" A year later, I saw the same dorky guy on TV. He had his own sitcom, and his name was Jerry Seinfeld.

Nooners were super depressing and sad. But any show in a room where they were still conducting some kind of business could bring you to a Demi Moore in *St. Elmo's Fire* state of mind.

I once had to perform at a school in New York at one of their eateries, which was not only still serving food but had a smoothie bar set up right next to the stage. Right. Next. To. The. STAGE. So they were synthesizing smoothies in a *blender* throughout my entire set.

"How many of you have a friend . . ."

VRRRRRRRRRRRRRRRRR

". . . who annoys you so much . . ."

VRRRRRRRRRRRRRRRRR

"... THAT YOU WANNA SLAM THEM IN THE FACE WITH A BLENDER?!?! Come. On. Really??"

It was a fucking nightmare. Everybody was eating and jibber-jabbering and no one even seemed to know I was on a stage performing comedy, except for one table of girls who were trying to pay attention. I could tell they felt sorry for me because they kept giving me encouraging smiles that said, *You can do it. Don't be afraid, li'l buddy!* The "venue"—I hesitate to call it that—had additional seating in an upstairs section, which only made the acoustics even more deafening. It kept getting louder and louder and louder until I finally stopped for a moment, watched the crowd for about twenty seconds and said:

"You know what? I get paid whether you listen to me or not. I just need to sit up here for another twenty minutes."

Then I heard a lone voice cry out from the balcony.

"That's the funniest shit you said all night!"

Thank you, sir. I finished my set and cried all the way back to the hotel.

I've never really had a plan to deal with hecklers. I still don't. I probably should. My thing is to just be like, "Okay, you wanna be a part of this show so bad? What do you have to say?" Nine times out of ten they spew some nonsense or talk themselves into a hole and I just give a sad condescending look and move on with the show.

Groups of guys, like frat boys, can be the most annoying. They spend the majority of their days trying to make each other laugh so by the time they get to my show they think *they're* the entertainment. Then if one says anything, they all want to chime in. If I clown 'em on how foolish they sound, what comes next is a litany of OHHHHHHHHHHHHS and DAAAAAAAAAAMNS and an hour of "Yo, she told you, bro, you gonna take that shit?"

Hey, guys, we're not having a fight. I didn't come here to challenge you—I'm at WORK. The fuck?! Then the obvious next statement is, "I don't come to your job and knock the dicks outta your mouths." But that just seems lazy and crass, and I like to consider myself a classy bitch.

The most challenging audience I ever had was at a SUNY school, I can't remember which one. I didn't know there were this many black people IN upstate New York, let alone at one school. They were mostly city kids and they were raucous or, as they say, "wilin' out." I got so nervous because I could tell right away that once they saw a black comedian they were ready for a Def Comedy Jam kind of show and that ain't what mamma was bringin'. I wasn't in the mood to battle with my audience. Two guys got escorted out before I even got on-stage, and I thought, *How am I gonna reel them in?*

But I got through it, and it wasn't that bad. I actually walked offstage proud of how I handled the crowd and dealt with the hecklers. But when I was ready to leave I went to grab my coat . . . and it was GONE. I had left it in a chair in the front row of the auditorium and someone stole that shit! It was the dead of winter and some ass clown lifted my fucking coat. It was a lime-green wool peacoat and I loved that goddamn coat. The following day, I had to go into New York City for a meeting at Comedy Central. They wondered how I was in New York in the dead of winter without a coat and perhaps for a second pitied me for being a peasant. I told them of my misfortune at SUNY and they kindly offered up a *Daily Show with Jon Stewart* jacket so that I might survive the rest of my tour without catching pneumonia.

I felt so good winning over that crowd but they sure as shit got the last laugh, sending me out into the tundra with no overcoat. I gotta tell you, New York crowds are no joke. Storytelling the way I do it can be hard there. My bits were long, woven anecdotes about family and friends. Some of my material had social commentary in it and some of it was just shit that annoyed me. But New York crowds were not easily impressed. They would stare up at me like, "What you got next?"

When I first started paying attention to stand-up comedians I noticed that New York comics were often very negative in their comedy and the New York audiences seemed to love it. So when I first started doing stand-up, I thought I had to be negative in order to win them over. I soon realized I wasn't good at the negative comedy. I made an attempt at "angry comic" but I'm not an angry person (usually). So I abandoned that shit and eventually found my voice.

I needed to be myself for sure, but if I was really gonna make it as a comedian, I'd have to suck it up and find a way to deal with what came at me. Sometimes the audience would be assholes, or the venue would be too loud. Sometimes there wouldn't even be a stage or a mic, like the time I had to perform in a dorm common area while all the students lay down, lounging around me in their pajamas. Was I supposed to tell jokes? Read them *Goodnight Moon*? Lead Light as a Feather, Stiff as a Board? What kind of hippie kumbaya shit was this?

Every city, every campus, had its own flavor, its own vibe, and I needed to adapt. I knew the East Coast was cynical because they had robbed me. The South was a little sleepy (that's my PC way of saying slow movin'), so I'd have to be more animated, which I'm not necessarily. My favorite audiences were in the Pacific Northwest and the Midwest because they liked sitting and listening to stories and they were POLITE and attentive.

But not quite as polite as the Mormons. I got booked at Snow College in Ephraim, Utah, which was so bumfuck nowhere, the directions were to drive two hundred miles straight on some road until you get to the stoplight. Which stoplight? THE stoplight. There was only one.

"We just had a ribbon-cutting ceremony for it," they told me.

Oh.

So I get to Snow College, and everyone is very nice. There were even parents in the audience who brought their kids. Now, I never tailor my act to a specific audience. I just write what I think is funny, whether you like it or not is your business, not mine. I've been doing stand-up for a long time and you hire me based on what you know I do. And I do what I do so if you don't like it, don't book me because I'm not changing my set.

But I took one look at my wholesome Mormon hosts and my set flashed through my mind.

- Jokes about a boyfriend named Jesus
- Skinny boyfriend bit, where I describe him being on top
- Lions having sex

Hmm, the lion bit might not go over well here in Utah*:

I recently saw a special on one of those nature channels about the lions of the Serengeti. Does anyone here know how a female lion signals to the male as to the end of a sexual encounter? She attacks him. She viciously swipes at his head and then tries to bite him in the neck. I'm watching this and thinking . . . what a coincidence because you know I'm the same way! It's like, alright already, back the hell up! But what's odd is the male, he's cool about it. He doesn't let it bother him. Because he knows in another few minutes she's gonna want his goods again. How does he know this? Because lions have sex EVERY. TWENTY. MINUTES *while the female's in heat. So, basically, she swings on him, looks at her watch twenty minutes later and is like, Alright, bring ya ass.* SEX. *Every. Twenty. Minutes. I'm watching this and I'm thinking,* What a coincidence, I'm the same way! *Okay, so they do the wild thing or the "wild kingdom" thing, as it may be, every twenty minutes while she's in heat. Let's say she's in heat for three days. That is 216 sexual episodes in seventy-two hours. Yet some of you self-proclaimed playas like to brag about doing it twice in an hour before slipping into a coma.*

What's wrong with this picture, ladies? I tend to believe that there will come a day when man- and animal kind dwell together on this planet in harmony. And there will be parties. Perhaps keggers, I don't know how it's gonna work. The males will be gathered around the keg talking about their

---

* Despite the fact that the state is apparently the nation's largest manufacturer of rubber chickens! Who knew?

conquests, their escapades, what have you. One guy will be like, Yo, blood, check it out. I hit it twice last night. Yuh. I knocked it out. *And the lion's gonna hear this and be like,* What, did it hurt when she smacked you in the head? Is that why you quit? You punk ass? You mama's boy? You li'l bitch?

But you have to be careful when you're talking about a man's performance. Cuz men get their egos bruised. That's why women have to stroke and massage . . . the male ego. You know, build it back up. I'm curious as to whether the lioness has to do this. Let's say her mate only can do it 215 times. Is she like, That's alright, Bob, it happens to every lion. You're still the king of my jungle. *Perhaps. But once she leaves that den and is hanging out with her girlfriends, it's a* WHOLE *different story.* 215 times, pshhh, he's losing it. I think I'm gonna start seeing Tony. You know, the tiger? Girl, I hear he is Grrrrrrrreeeeeat!

Yeah, no.

I couldn't do anything sex-related or cuss. They were way too conservative. So, in this one case, for these nice people, I changed my set. After the show, I assumed they loved my act because they lined up to give me great big bear hugs good-bye like we were gonna be besties forever. When I got back to my hotel room, I went to take off my coat (a NEW coat) and noticed something in my left pocket. I reached into the pocket and found a *Book of Mormon.* One of my new "besties" had surreptitiously slipped it in there but not before highlighting several passages.

God bless 'em.

I had so many GTFO moments on the road. Like the time

I did a show at a military school in Roswell, New Mexico. The soldiers were a great audience, actually super well-mannered, too (they had to be or they'd have to get down and give me twenty). But anyone who's ever heard of Roswell knows that its claim to fame is that a UFO supposedly crashed there in 1947. Now I don't have such a big ego that I think we're alone in this universe. I guess I believe in extraterrestrials, I can't say they've made it to Earth yet. So, I kinda laughed about the multitude of Martians painted on the glass storefronts all through town. I was like, *Wow, they are really committed.* Took that alien hook and ran with it. No, what freaked me out more about Roswell was the desolate, barren feel of the place. It felt more likely that I'd find myself kidnapped and forced to make meth in a *Breaking Bad* RV than abducted and whisked away to planet Caprica where my face and body would be used as the template for the fourteenth cylon humanoid model (waddap, *Battlestar Galactica* peeps?). Aliens were the least of my problems.

I've been everywhere and done stand-up in every state and corner of this country. And this was before iPhones and Siri and the Google map app. Cell phones were just becoming popular and there was barely a single G of service for huge swaths of red states. They'd drop this black girl in the dead of night in the middle of nowhere, with just a cheap rental car—like a purple Ford Aspire—and an Enterprise tear-away map, the real paper kind. Trust me when I say this was terrifying, especially when I was in the Deep South by myself and was too scared to go into a gas station to ask for directions. People would stare at me like they knew I wasn't from them parts. Those were some scary times.

If I didn't have my own rental car, sometimes I'd be abandoned at sketchy hotels near six-lane highways and forgotten about until it was time to pick me up for the show. Best-case scenario, the hotel would have a Steak 'n Shake and I'd just eat breakfast, lunch, and dinner* there until someone came to fetch me. Worst-case scenario, I'd subsist on Pop-Tarts from the vending machine. I remember one particular hotel was so scary, I didn't even take my shoes off and I slept in my clothes. The door didn't touch the ground so there was an inch of space through which any number of bugs and critters could crawl and axe murderers could peek through. Or escaped convicts. I turned on the TV and the news actually reported that the local prison had had a breakout and residents shouldn't answer the door "if you don't know who it is." What in the actual fuck?

I stayed in shitty hotels like that a few times. My least favorite was in San Angelo, Texas, "The Place to Come for Good Times." Or not. Because it was so isolated, there was absolutely nothing to do. So I stayed in my hotel room all day doing absolutely nothing. It was a "No Smoking" room. You know how I knew it was a "No Smoking" room? Because there was an *ashtray* with a NO SMOKING sticker on the outside bottom of it. If you turned it over, I guess it was a *smoking* room? There was a light switch on the wall that controlled the air-conditioning. To prevent guests from flipping the switch, they put a Band-Aid on it and wrote in pen, DO NOT TURN OFF/AIR COND. I'm not sure if it was clean or used, I didn't look, all I know is using a bandage as signage was some

---

* I haven't eaten Steak 'n Shake since. People are geeked we now have it in Los Angeles and I couldn't care less.

raggedy-ass shit. Y'all couldn't go get some masking tape? Any kind of tape? A Post-it? C'mon.

Most of the time on these road trips, I was all by myself. Which was fine. I wasn't tryna get drunk with a buncha college students and miss my flight home. I wasn't Mötley Crüe, partying all night after my shows and hooking up with my groupies and having drug-fueled orgies. I didn't have any groupies, though one time a fan did find me at my hotel . . . because it was the only hotel in town.

The only time I ever went out with fans was after a show in the Louisiana bayou. The student programming board member was a cute guy who invited me to hang with his fraternity. So I said fuck it and drove to a crazy country bar to meet up with him and his frat brothers. But they weren't two-stepping to Garth Brooks in that honky-tonk (more puns!). These boys were singing and dancing to Master P. I hadn't even heard these songs before. I barely knew who Master P was when they told me what song was playing. I've never seen so many white boys feelin' Southern rap. I mean feeeeeling it, down in their souls. It was fascinating to watch. It was like some kind of bizzaro world in which preppy was all of a sudden thug. I was dying.

Speaking of dying (#terriblesegue), the more I flew, the more I loathed and feared it. I had a few close calls in turbo-props so small and sketchy, they felt like the *Memphis Belle**

---

* The only reason I'm familiar with the *Memphis Belle* (the United States Air Force B-17 heavy bomber) is because the film *Memphis Belle* is one of my favorite movies. This is a big deal because I hate war films. And yet it holds a special place in my heart . . . probably because Harry Connick Jr. is in it and I luuuurve him.

in World War II. Once on a flight out of Sioux Falls, South Dakota, several other passengers and I noticed smoke in the cabin. It was an obscenely early flight so it was still dark outside. The only lights on in the cabin were the overhead lights, and we could see the smoke swirling in the overhead beams. One of my co-passengers went to the cockpit and frantically told the pilots (this was before 9/11, when you could just pop on by and say "What up").

"Oh yeah, we're aware of it," they said nonchalantly, while the rest of us wrote good-bye letters to our families. "It should dissipate soon." 😑

I suffered through a fierce wind-shear landing in Chicago that left me in tears and prompted me to call my agent from the terminal and demand that he cancel the rest of my shows. I sat next to a girl on a flight that was so turbulent it caused her and three other passengers to projectile vomit. She was holding the fucking barf bag but didn't even have time to put it up to her mouth! Yes, some of it got ON me. It was horrifying. I tried to be cool about it because I flew enough to understand her pain, and especially since she apologized profusely, but there was vomit ON MY HAND. It was NOT cool.

I remember the time I ate crab cakes in a landlocked city somewhere in the Midwest (Note to self: Never order crab thousands of miles from the nearest ocean) and I got violent food poisoning. I threw up for hours and had such stomachwrenching diarrhea that I swore I could see the genesis of abs by morning. I had to get on a flight that morning and I was NOT well. I was pouring sweat and my skin was gray. My flight was delayed and I had to sit at the gate closest to the ladies' room because . . . duh. It was utter hell. The delay caused me to miss my connection so I had to stand in line with a slew of other travelers to rebook for the next day and be assigned a hotel room for the night. By the time I got to the front of the line all I could do was cry. I was so pathetic and the ticket agent felt so sorry for me that she gave me a voucher for the Hilton RIGHT in the airport. I continued my dance with the porcelain tureen until the wee hours of the night. I've never felt so abused and empty.

I'm sorry. That was a brutal description but it's necessary to understand why I hate doing stand-up on the road and why I'm not so eager to return to life on the road. It was a Catch-22. I was on the road making money (and at that time in my life it was GOOD money) but I wasn't in town available to audition and make moves in the direction of where I had planned to go.

Don't get me wrong. I like making people laugh. That's what I enjoy. It makes me happy to see people happy and having a good time. But everything else about it made me wanna throw myself off a building. I'd rather walk the Arctic tundra with no water or sustenance in winter without a coat, which I'd have to do anyway since those fuckers at SUNY stole my shit.

Chapter Eight

I Think I Might Be Lazy

I think I might be lazy. I know I just said that, but it's easier to repeat it than to come up with something new. And THAT is one of many instances of my laziness.

Other indicators of my laziness?

1. In the last two years I've shaved my legs three times.

2. I sit down when heating up leftovers . . . in the microwave.

3. I've already decided that if I ever get engaged, I'm registering for Dixie products. Because I think we can all agree that dishes are some bullshit.

I don't know when or how it happened. I went to a good school, graduated pre-med with ambitions of becoming a neurosurgeon, but I somehow ended up with a job that allows me to sleep till early evening. I put in a maximum of one hour per shift, and most of the time, I can drink on the job.

Maybe it's not just me.

4. Has anyone else ever let their toenails go to a point where it's uncomfortable to wear your own shoes?

5. Have you ever encountered an OUT OF ORDER sign on an escalator and thought: *What the hell is this bullshit? I didn't sign up for stairs.* Have you ever taken an elevator up one floor . . . at the gym?

I just found out my gym has a sauna. I had no idea because after seven years of membership, I still haven't taken the tour. I won't take the tour because I know if I do they'll expect me to use the stairs and . . . I don't do stairs. When I go to the gym I do two things:

6. I ride the recumbent bike (that's the stationary bike with the bucket seat. It's like doing cardio in the passenger side of a Pontiac Fiero).

7. I weight train using the Life Fitness machines. I use the Life Fitness machines, as opposed to free weights, because most of the Life Fitness machines have seats.

In fact, the only time you'll catch me *standing* at the gym is if you get on the elevator with me.

Now the obvious question here would be, if I'm really that lazy, why did I join a gym? Because I'm not completely inert. I realize that I've gotten as big as I need to get. I'm not looking to make history. As much as I crave the spotlight, entry into the *Guinness World Records* is not something I covet. I certainly don't want get to a point where my only viable means of transportation is a crane outside my bedroom window. Gas prices are already kicking my ass. I don't know what it costs to run John Deere equipment but I'm pretty sure I can't afford it. So, in truth, I joined a gym not for health reasons but because it would be fiscally irresponsible of me not to.

That said, is there little doubt that I am indeed lazy? I've been known to:

8. Sit on an escalator.

I don't know what it is about sitting down but it's VERY IMPORTANT to me. It makes me feel like I can relax. The deciding factor in choosing my condo was that the shower in the master bath had a seat . . . BUILT IN. I'm not afraid to tell you folks . . .

9. I shower sitting down. Don't worry, I stand up to get the hot spots but, for the most part, I parks it when showering.

Awhile back I was watching *MTV Cribs* and they showed Mariah Carey's bathroom and she had a flat-screen TV at the foot of her tub and I thought *Man, I should put a flat-screen in my bathroom. Not only would I get to relax, I'd get to behold the delight that is television.*

Anyway, I actually started going through the logistics, in my head, of how to mount a flat-screen next to my toilet. But something gave me pause and that something was the fact that it doesn't take much for me to slip into dormant mode. I'm one of those people who go to the bathroom in the middle of the night and end up sleeping on the pot for a lil' bit. You ever do that?

10. Catch a few zzz's while you pees?

Don't look at me like that. I know there are at least a handful of guys here that do it, too. How else do you explain your disgusting bachelor bathrooms? I'm *hoping* that semiunconsciousness plays a part in the "golden moat" phenomenon.

Anyway, it started to become clearer that this *probably* wasn't such a good idea for an admitted sloth. With my luck I'd be in the shower, *sitting*, getting my "cleanse on" while watching MTV, and some marathon would come on and I'd have to call it a day. Next thing ya know I'm as wrinkled as Hugh Hefner's nuts and I've missed two car payments. Because if there is one thing a slacker should not get caught up in, it's a marathon . . . and more to the point . . .

11. Get caught up in a cable-network marathon. That shit will reel you in. My guilty pleasure was *My Super Sweet 16*. OMG that shit is like manna from heaven. Why? Where else can you find such an obvious display of overindulgence and narcissism? Other than the waiting room of a Beverly Hills plastic surgeon? Each episode is more ridiculous than the last. These ungrateful little bastards are rude, selfish, ungracious, and show little to no respect for their parents, who are either pushovers or more than willing to spoil their demon spawn with expensive clothes and luxury cars. I can't help but think *My God, why weren't my parents rich?* Seriously, this one girl demanded three dresses for "costume changes" at her party. Each dress cost more than $1,000 so her parents bought her four . . . just in case!

You know what I remember about shopping for an outfit for my sixteenth birthday? My father looking at a price tag and going, "Forty dollars for some jeans? You must think we're related to Sergio Forlenté! You gon' get some Lee jeans and like 'em."

I'm like, "Forlenté? It's Valente, dad, Sergio Valente."

He was like, "Unless there's some kind of phenomenal sales eventé, that forty-dollar price tag is gonna preventé you from gettin' 'em. What's wrong with these gauchos? And they come with a belt."

"It's braided."

"I know, right?" he said. "Sharp."

I think it is safe to assume that if you invite me to participate in anything that is described as aerobic, energetic, or vigorous, my RSVP will be in the negative:

no

unh-unh

not

nah

can't

won't

nyet

non

unavailable

sorry

I don't even want to play Monopoly anymore, the most boring, sedentary game ever invented. But I will play *McDonald's* Monopoly. Why? Even though it's redonkulous and tedious peeling those little freakin' game pieces off, I'm saving those little bastards in the hopes of winning one *meellion* dollars. Because lazy people will do anything that offers an opportunity to take the year off. I have a million of these fuckin' things in my apartment and at any given time I have at least four in my wallet.

I feel like it could happen, and with minimal effort on my part. I will go to McDonald's. There's a drive-through window so I don't even have to get out of the car. I get food that has already been prepared because, it's safe to assume, I don't like to cook. And then all I have to do is peel off the little game pieces for a chance at not having to work. Of course I haven't won, and I've rationalized that McDonald's is not gonna let someone from LA win. I mean, why would they? Most of us already don't work. I'm convinced that someone from Idaho's gonna get my million and fuck up my sabbatical. My friend Rachel says that my matches are probably on the East Coast so I've taken to emailing friends around the country and asking if they'll send me their Monopoly game pieces. If I win I'll split it with them. This seems like a lot of effort, but for a chance to take the *YEAR* off? It's worth it. Lazy people believe in luck. Why? Because it's easier than devising a ten-year plan or setting up an IRA.

You can also probably infer that I'm not particularly fond of the prefixes cardio- or hyper-. Lazy people aren't the adventurous types. We don't want to be involved with anything that includes the words:

escapade

excursion

expedition

explore

frolic

journey

romp

sightsee

survey

tour

traverse

trek

So, don't invite me out on Halloween. I don't want to go trick-or-treating or to your Halloween party, especially one where costumes are "required." Halloween is a holiday that requires/demands effort. I get annoyed picking out clothes for the gym.

12. I'm not dressing up for your costume party.

Nope, not gonna happen. The last Halloween party I went to, I spent the better part of the night dodging sloppy drunks on precarious footing. It went something like this: "Don't get makeup on me. Could you not? Sir, your mascara."

I don't like Halloween because it's amateur night. It's

drunk girls who use the holiday to be naked in public and drunk guys who use it to get away with dressing in drag. Really, guy? You put on a dress, an Indian headdress, and some lip gloss and now you're Cher? That's lazy. But like bullshit rookie lazy. If you're gonna be lazy, BE LAZY. Do what I do. Last Halloween when people asked me what I was, I told 'em—a minority.

I particularly hate Halloween in a city that has a substantial gay community. Because outside of Pride, Halloween is a high holy day for the gays and with that comes another freaking parade. And with a parade comes traffic, which means planning travel routes.

13. Rerouting takes effort, and I think we all know where I stand on that front.

And I'm not driving anywhere if the parking situation stresses me out. I'm jealous of the handicapped. Because they get all the great parking. Up-front and center, right at the mall entrance. No doing laps in the parking deck on Black Friday. No stalking that slow-ass couple whose look of trepidation should've clued you in that they have no earthly idea of where they parked their Chevy Malibu. And why is it that the handicapped get to park so close? It's not like they have to hike the never-ending trek that is the parking structure. They get to "roll" in and half the time someone else is doing the pushing. Leave the upfront parking for old people (who walk) and me.

14. The giddiest months of my life were the three months I had a temporary handicap-parking placard.

Those days I went to the mall two and three times a day. These days I'm relegated to shopping online. If it weren't for the internet, I'd still be wearing acid-wash jeans and off-the-shoulder sweatshirts.

15. By the way, I love playing on the computer in my bed.

Sedentary people often do. I love playing on my computer almost as much as I like . . .

16. . . . napping, so you can imagine my joy the day I got a wireless laptop. That's when I knew without a doubt that Jesus loved me. Why else would he make getting out of bed "optional"?

17. I pay bills in bed.

18. I send Evites and do my Christmas shopping in bed.

19. I check my Facebook page and order from Grubhub in bed.

20. And I'm not ashamed to tell ya, I google myself in bed (in more ways than one).

But mostly I send my mother links to Snopes.com. The woman believes every email that crosses her desktop. She still thinks that flashing her headlights at night to an oncoming car is gonna get her "clipped" in some gang initiation. I'm like, "You're not gonna get *clipped*. You live in suburban central Jersey . . . at the beach. You'll be aw-ite."

The internet has got her more paranoid than ever. I have

to constantly reassure her: "Mom, I don't use Glade candles so my apartment's not gonna catch fire, nor do I use my cell phone when pumping gas. And you can inform your prayer circle that the nine-year-old Penny Brown is not missing. Yeah, I saw her on *Good Morning America* with her three kids. She was pleading with the internet community to stop forwarding her third-grade school picture." I don't mind that she forwards inspirational haikus or the scripture of the day from e-ministry . . . well, I *do* mind but I can't, in good conscience, hate on the word of God. The thing is, my mom's one of those people who thinks forwarding an email constitutes a correspondence.

21. And when I don't reply she'll call me.

"Did you get my email?"
"Yes."
"Why didn't you write me back?"
"Because I'm tired of telling you that Bill Gates is NOT gonna send you a hundred dollars for every email you forward. The 'Nigerian prince' asking for your help is a scam. Ciara is not a man, and neither Sinbad nor Urkel is dead. STOP SENDING ME THIS SHIT! Or you're gonna find your ass in my spam folder." As thinking adults you all can probably see that relegating your mother to your spam folder is but a short hop, skip, and a jump away from a retirement community for continuing care. Just a heads-up, Deborah.

22. Anyway, I love being in bed.

One time, I was lying in my bed flicking through my On Demand channels and I accidentally clicked on *Fast and Furious: Tokyo Drift*. Just as I was about to hit the exit button, the phone rang and scared me and I dropped the remote under my bed. WAY UNDER MY BED. Soooo now I'm watching *Fast & Furious: Tokyo Drift* and it begins with the rich overprivileged jock getting pissed because the new guy, who just happens to be from the wrong side of the tracks, is talking to his girl. This behavior at movie high schools is equivalent to a capital crime and serves as a challenge to one's jock-dom. How are we to know who has the bigger dick? With a drag race, of course. So the kid from the wrong side of the tracks—let's call him Kevin Bacon—says, "I only race for pink slips."

The jock looks at him like, *Are you kidding me?* 'Cause he's driving an $80,000 Viper and Bacon is driving, like, a banana-yellow '71 Monte Carlo. Now I'm not one to take the jock's side, especially when he's being played by Zachery Ty Bryan (the bigheaded older son from *Home Improvement*). But I see his point. That's like playing high-stakes poker; I'm using $1,000-dollar chips and you're playing with Lay's potato chips. Realizing that a pink slip is an uneven trade, the girlfriend—let's call her Lori Singer—chimes in, "How 'bout me? Winner . . . gets . . . me."

Really? Um, the '80s called, they want ALL this BULLSHIT back.

23. And, yes, I watched the entire movie because I just could not bring myself to get out of bed in an attempt to find my remote.

My bed's REALLY high off the floor. And not only that, it is really dusty under there. My people* aren't meticulous housekeepers.

24. In fact, the last time I did try to tackle the dust under my bed, I pulled something in my back and was stuck in bed for four days. Only the lazy can incur an immobilizing injury while dusting.

Lazy people don't jump right up out of bed over something trivial/banal/superfluous. My bed would have to literally be on fire for me to get out of it. Here's a hypothetical: It's 4:00 a.m. on a Sunday morning and I'm experiencing the sweetest, most blissful slumber I've had in weeks. What would be worse?

> The blaring alarm of a neighbor's car so piercing it stirs latent homicidal tendencies within you?
> -OR-
> The incessant chirp of a dying battery in your smoke detector?

I gotta go with the dying battery because there's a special kind of madness that comes with knowing that you and only you can silence your tormentor, if only you had a 9-volt battery. There were piles of 9-volt batteries at the 99-cent store just waiting to get picked up but you walked right past them, opting instead for the combination lock and envelopes. Yes,

---

* My people are lazy people.

this happened to me. And I found myself lying there squealing like Nancy Kerrigan, "Whyyy meee?" And more important, why 9-volt? Why not C or AA? Because I've got plenty of those. I've got enough batteries to power every flashlight from here to Canoga Park. When I couldn't take the chirping anymore, I finally got up to look for a battery, KNOWING I hadn't bought a 9-volt battery in two years, which just happens to coincide with the chirping death of my last 9-volt. You know what I found? Two unopened twelve-packs of AAA batteries.

Why would I possibly need twenty-four AAA batteries? Because my being prepared for the very real possibility that every single one of my remote controls might become inoperable at the same time takes precedence over the likelihood of me perishing in a fiery death.

So what's the moral of this story? Honestly?

25. I'm too lazy to come up with one.

Chapter Nine

Food, Water, Oxygen, Television

I take television very seriously. And by seriously, I mean with the kind of dedication and loyalty you might find in a Scientologist or a golden retriever. I'm not just your average binger, using a show for my own amusement for one intense weekend and then tossing it aside like a pen without ink or a pro athlete's first wife. I get invested, almost to my own detriment. I let shows emotionally affect me to the point where it almost breaks me. And even then I stick with it like a battered wife who foolishly believes it won't hurt me again.

There has not been an episode of *So You Think You Can Dance* that I haven't cried to. With a title like *So You Think You Can Dance* one might think there is nothing but joy and unadulterated jubilation associated with this program. After all, it's fucking dancing. Oh but no, my dear friends. This is far from the reality that is *SYTYCD*. When's the last time you saw someone on the dance floor at a party and it brought you to the kind of tears where you heave with grief-induced hyperventilation? Never? Well, this is my experience every time

I watch this so-called dance show, whether it's a piece choreographed to honor the life and death of the choreographer's friend who died too soon from a swift and unforgiving cancer or a pop locker performing a lyrical number like a Nobel laureate reading his prize-winning poem. That is how a television *dance* competition does *me*.

Hi, my name is Retta and I'm a teleholic. It first started when I was a toddler. PBS was my pusher and *Sesame Street* was my gateway drug. I have been in love with/addicted to television ever since I can remember. Aside from the love of family, it has been the one constant in my life. Whether I'm happy or sad, feeling motivated or stagnant, I always turn to television for balance. For a sense of relief. For a sense of normalcy. It keeps me steady when I need it and brings me up when I'm low. It's my own personal serotonin.

If I love something on TV, I will rewatch and revisit it in order to relive my initial viewing experience. I've seen *Sex and the City*, *Will & Grace*, *Cougar Town*, and, I'm not ashamed to admit it, *Parks and Rec*, I don't know how many times. I watched the entire *West Wing* series twice in a row, back-to-back. That's fourteen seasons, 310 episodes with nothing in between because apparently Aaron Sorkin *does* something for me.

Even genres I thought were not my cup of tea have gotten me on board, including sci-fi (*Orphan Black*, *Battlestar Galactica*, *Fringe*, *The Expanse*), zombies (*The Walking Dead*), and vampires (*Angel*, *True Blood*, *The Vampire Diaries*, *Kindred*). I shouldn't be too surprised by my vampy faves because I did love the Count on *Sesame Street*. The one genre I haven't been able to get into is cartoons. I liked them as a kid but I just can't vibe with them as an adult.

I'm also that person who recognizes someone from another show and feels the need to let everyone know, whether it be sending a tweet or telling someone actually in the room. "Oh shit! Mrs. Patmore! Who knew she could be a crime boss?!'" said I while watching an episode of *The Catch*.

You can call me IMDBeyotch.

I luh my programs. Highbrow (*Downton Abbey*) and low-brow (*Laguna Beach*). Antiheroes (Tony Soprano) and unlikely heroes (Walter White). Comedies (*Modern Family*) and especially dramedies (*Freaks and Geeks, Orange Is the New Black, Shameless, Gilmore Girls, Californication, Weeds, Veronica Mars*, I could go fucking onnnnn). And, ooh yes, procedural doc shows, like *Grey's Anatomy*. I get to live vicariously through these characters. It's as though their experiences are mine, with all the breakthroughs and none of the lost patients! Mc-Dreamy was the ultimate because, you know, neurosurgeon and all, but then (spoiler alert) he gets into a car wreck? WTF??

Watching TV is my happy place (soul-crushing deaths of my favorite characters aside). As a latchkey kid, I watched television in the mornings before school as I ate my cereal and then when I got home from school I immediately did my homework and I watched back-to-back shows until bedtime. I ate dinner within earshot of the television because I just couldn't miss anything.* When *Happy Days* was over—when The Fonz said "Ayyyyyy"—I knew it was time to hit the hay. My parents didn't need to read me *Go the Fuck to Sleep*. I *knew*

---

* My mother now has a television in the kitchen, so I no longer miss out on the visuals when eating at the kitchen table.

I was going the fuck to sleep. At 9:00 p.m. sharp, my butt better be in that bed. But one night I actually looked at the clock when *Happy Days* was over and it read 8:30. Hol' up. Do my eyes deceive me? I walked over to my parents' bedroom, perplexed.

"Mom, it's only 8:30," I said incredulously.

"I know," was my mother's response.

"I always go to bed after *Happy Days*!"

"I know. I just thought you were tired," my mom replied.

What the hell? I had been missing THIRTY MINUTES OF TELEVISION every Tuesday for years! When I realized I would finally get to watch *Laverne & Shirley*, a show whose ads I'd seen for years, it was like Christmas morning! I had an extra half hour to stay up and bask in the comedy of goofy besties Laverne and Shirley aaand Lenny and Squiggy.

I don't know if my parents knew how many sexual innuendos I was being bombarded with on a nightly basis in the Swingin' '70s, between Len and Squig's lascivious looks and all that braless jigglin' going on at The Regal Beagle on *Three's Company*. My mom and dad might have been strict about a lot of things, but they let me watch endless amounts of unsupervised television. Seems like everybody did back then. I watched from dawn 'til dusk. At breakfast, I got on board *The Great Space Coaster* while I ate my cereal-water concoction. After school, I watched *General Hospital* or *The Munsters* reruns. At night, I was ready for primetime, and that could be anything from *All in the Family*, which was way over my head, to *Welcome Back, Kotter*.

Our TVs were our babysitters back in my latchkey days, the equivalent of our smartphones today. And just like how now they say our phones are destroying our eyes and brains and social skills, turning us into zombies, the same thing was said about the boob tube. It was the "vast wasteland."* I respectfully disagree with that assessment. I got a lot of beneficial shit from my TV watching as an impressionable young lass. Looking back, I can see my future from what I was enjoying on TV. I see what I wanted for MY life based on what shows I was obsessed over. The shows weren't rotting my brain; they were aspirational.

First, I discovered that I had a particular affinity for shows where people had nice homes. *Sanford and Son* stressed me out because of all the junk. I can't take a cluttered home, and the fact that they literally lived in a house filled with junk made me want to burn it to the ground.† Why would I want to watch *Good Times*, where they lived in a sparse, mostly beige, low-income project, when I could watch *I Dream of Jeannie* and fantasize about living in a bright glass bottle filled with comfy, cozy, colorful, oversized cushions?! I didn't appreciate *Sanford and Son* or even *M*A*S*H*, the Emmy Award–winning comedy about the Korean War, because I didn't like the color palette. So much dust, so little flora. *M*A*S*H* was all dirt or military green, and I didn't like green. I liked red and purple and orange and gold, like Jeannie's bottle. I also liked Jeannie's ability to make thangs happen (and appear) with the blink of an eye and a nod of the

---

* According to a famous quote by former FCC chairman Newton N. Minow.

† Fun fact: My mother is a "keeper of things." Tchotchkes, tchotchkes everywhere. I am moments away from submitting her for A&E's *Hoarders*.

head. It's the same reason I liked Tabitha on *Bewitched*. I was all about twitching my nose—*twinkle twinkle twinkle!*—and breakfast was made or a new vacuum cleaner would appear. The closest I can get to that kind of magic is Postmates and Amazon Prime, and trust me, I use the shit out of those.

I longed to live in a sitcom, but not just any sitcom. I yearned for a pristine, pretty world (the infamous afghan on the raggedy *Roseanne* couch gave me the shivers). The place I wanted to live in most was *The Brady Bunch* house in California. I'd never seen a house like that in my life! So open and clean! *The Brady Bunch* also taught me how to deal with all the motherfucking people in my house. At our place, we were piled up in tiny rooms. The Brady kids had the three-and-three situation, but their rooms were HUGE compared to mine. I remember Greg being so pressed to move to the attic and I was like, "Dude, I'll take your place in your room any day! I don't know what the fuck y'all are complaining about."

My home today is relatively spotless and mostly uncluttered* at all times. Uncluttered includes it being free of people. It's odd because I always want to be around people. Perhaps it's because I grew up in a house filled with people. I always *think* I want to entertain guests. I go out of my way to make my place inviting. I provide my guests with a fluffy guest robe like nice hotels do. I even have a basket of white rolled hand

---

* My guest-room closet hides a multitude of sins, and by "sins" I mean acquired swag from Hollywood events and well-intentioned but sorely misguided birthday gifts.

towels like they have at fancy hotels. My guest bathroom is nicer than the one in my master bedroom. But when I do have guests, it only takes about two days for me to remember how nice it was NOT having guests. I never had that experience growing up. There was always *another* cousin moving in. It's probably why I was so bent outta shape when cousin Oliver showed up at the Bradys' split-level mid-century modern masterpiece because I knew from having random extended family move in for only God knows how long. The house was more crowded, the lines for the bathroom were longer, food ran out much quicker, and there were more fights over what to watch on the television and thus more reasons for my parents to be annoyed with the whole lot of us. Same thing when cousin Pam came to stay with the Huxtables on *The Cosby Show*. I mean, what the fuuuuuuck?*

Aside from the encroachment of cousin Pam, I loved everything about *The Cosby Show* (emphasis on the *show*—I'm not about to get into Bill Cosby the person here; I'll need another book deal for that hot mess). Like so many kids, I wanted to be a Huxtable because:

1. How cool would it have been to have a hippy-dippy, funky sister like Denise, Lisa Bonet's character? I've never had a sister. She could've saved me from so much boy-inflicted heartache.

2. The in-house entertainment!

---

* Don't get me wrong, I realize that it is a great blessing to be able to provide a home for those who need it. My mother is a GD saint. But I was a teen and wanted my privacy. Sue me.

3. And the parents?! The dad's a doctor (which I knew
for sure I was gonna be)? Mom's a lawyer? I meeeeean
BALLER, right? I just remember seeing a black family
in a house* and thinking, *If that ain't livin'!*

Another favorite was *The Jeffersons*. I liked that they were
affluent, yes. And they lived in a de-luxe apartment in the sky.
But, more important, they had a yellow couch with orange
accents. Finally, somebody with style! I thought it was hilarious that George couldn't understand his neighbors. He just
didn't get how a fly girl like Helen Willis (played by Roxie
Roker, the mother of one of the coolest rock stars there is,
Lenny Kravitz) could be married to, nay, in love with, Tom,
the epitome of the goofy white guy. I didn't get it either! Not
because Tom was a white guy. I loved white guys! In high
school white boys were my jam! And, to clarify, I don't ex-
clusively covet white men. I have enjoyed the company of a
rainbow assortment of gentlemen in my modest sexual history. But in high school that's what was around me.

My mother, a proud African who only became a U.S. cit-
izen when I graduated college because my father was fed up
with the drama at customs when they traveled, used to shake
her head and laugh. "Ay yah. I jus know you will marray a
white man. At lease I kno I will half beautuhfaux granchi-
ren." (My mother's accent is a point of pride. She has no interest in losing it.) The only thing she didn't appreciate was
the fact that I would not suffer the agony she had to endure

---

* I know it was a brownstone, but it was a house as far as I was concerned. There were two floors, for God's sake.

when doing my hair. I know most kids can be difficult when getting their hair done, and I was particularly problematic. I had African hair that wanted nothing to do with American hairstyles and, as a result, I was a handful for Deb. Brushing it out was a nightmare, unless I got it processed. I remember my mother hot-combing my hair and using Vigorol. It smelled horrendous, and to this day I still don't know its purpose. She resented that I would never know her struggle if I had mixed-race babies. My mother deserves a shout-out for managing to make me look cute in that classic '70s hairstyle for girls— six little pigtails adorned with those Kabanger-looking hair ties and barrettes hanging on the ends of the twists.

Anyway, that was a bit of a sidetrack. My point is, I liked white boys so I wasn't upset about Helen and Tom as a couple. What I didn't understand, though: How was she attracted to Tom Willis? George Jefferson was so thrown by her liking a white man. I was just mad she liked that *particular* white man! I was more of a Jason Bateman in *Silver Spoons* kind of gal (I was twelve).*

TV was about escapism for me. I was living *Good Times* in real life, and let me tell you, it most definitely wasn't as good of a time as *The Love Boat*. Everybody's on vacation and there's a pool on the friggin' boat—how bad could it be? I used to daydream about what I would ask for if I was lucky enough to meet Mr. Roarke and Tattoo on *Fantasy Island* after disembarking de plane. What would I do? I'll tell you what I'd

---

* We can't really go by my taste in men. I also had a thing for *Charles in Charge*'s Scott Baio. Who knew he'd be an outspoken Trump supporter? Like, totally gag me with a spoon.

do. Live in a big-ass freestanding house with no frickin' cousins in it.

But there was no such thing as a free lunch on *Fantasy Island*. There was always a price to pay. Nobody on that show ever got exactly what they wanted and there was always some lesson learned. Like, they might gift me my sick house with an infinity pool and claw-foot bathtub, but it'd probably be haunted by the ghost of a bride-to-be who insisted I wear a strapless dress to teach me that being a selfish loner is NEVER the answer.

Hey, just because I crave peace and quiet doesn't mean I'm a hermit. Quite the opposite—I'm a major girls' girl, despite or maybe due to the fact that I grew up with two brothers. I love hanging with my girlfriends, my lifeblood. And if you look at the long list of shows I liked as a kid, starting with *Laverne & Shirley*, there was a running theme—sisters before misters. I was obsessed with *The Facts of Life*, about four teen gals—Blair, Jo, Tootie, and Natalie—from four completely different backgrounds living together in a dorm at an all-girls' boarding school. I was like, how cool would it be to go to school and live with girls! ALL GIRLS! Then, when I realized I'd have to share a room with six girls, I wanted to shoot myself in the face.

But six girls sharing one mirror in a tiny bathroom. Imagine the hair clogs. Even so, it would *still* be way better than living with two guys, like on *The Odd Couple*. I hated that show because (1) Oscar was a disgusting pig, and (2) they weren't really friends! They were always fussing at each other and definitely didn't have each other's backs.

I appreciate and hold sacred that quality in best friends.

Hands down, number one on my long list of great TV shows is *Sex and the City*. I loved the friendship between Carrie, Miranda, Charlotte, and Samantha because it was so real. Some of my favorite episodes are when Carrie and Miranda got into fights. They are uncomfortable to watch because they remind you of what it's like to argue with your bestie but they always end up making up. Doesn't matter how mad they were or what they were fighting about, they always show up for their friend.* Those real moments meant a lot to me. They always had each other's back.

I lived vicariously through those four gals. I went through a really broke time, but it was okay because I felt like when they went out for fancy cosmos, I went out for fancy cosmos. When they went to fancy parties, I was right there with them. When they went shopping for Manolos, I got to virtually shop, too. When they had sex . . . well, let's just say I learned a lot. Their openness and honesty about sex was refreshing. The series broadcast happened to coincide with a time in my life when I was becoming more sexually aware and figuring out who I was and being more open about sex. I so related to Miranda's work ethic and dedication to excellence in her career, to Carrie's commitment to succeeding on her own, and to Samantha's unabashed sexual independence, and there

---

* S2Ep1: "Take Me Out to the Ball Game"—Even though Miranda stormed out of breakfast, she's the first person Carrie calls when she's sad about Big.

S3Ep18: "Cock-a-Doodle-Do"—They both call each other out about their personal shortcomings when it comes to men but they later admit to their issues and apologize.

was even a point when I had baby pangs when Charlotte longed to be a mother.

I didn't even realize it until I sat down to write this chapter, but television has been a mirror into my life and what I hold important. I thought I'd just write something funny about all the shows I'm obsessed with. But the more I thought about it, the more I realized it was all interrelated. I bet if you thought about it, too, you'd see some connections between your own life and your TV life. Unless you're one of those people who doesn't own a TV and, if so, I don't even want to know you.

I have an affinity toward shows about friends who had aesthetically pleasing lodgings and apparently enjoy observing the wealthy in their beautiful homes no matter the decade. In the '70s it was *Diff'rent Strokes*, the '80s *Dynasty*, the '90s *Beverly Hills, 90210*, and the '00s *Dirty Sexy Money*. I like shows where everybody gets along. That's why I can't really watch a lot of reality TV. All the in-fighting makes me uncomfortable and I find myself getting angry at people I don't know. It brings out the Judgey McJudgerson in me. Yelling at TV personalities, telling them what they should and should not be doing. Too stressful. I'd rather work shit out! I'm not saying I don't like the real dark stuff, like *The Shield* or *The Wire*, or stuff that makes you cry on purpose, like *SYTYCD*, cuz I do. But I tend to watch those kinds of shows when I'm not feeling quite like myself. The vibe I prefer in my life 24/7 is friendship and laughter. The misunderstandings and ridiculous assumptions on shows like *Three's Company*, *Laverne & Shirley*, *NewsRadio*, *Cougar Town*, *Will & Grace*, *Scrubs*, and

Cheers. You'd be hard-pressed to not enjoy the silliness of these iconic TV shows.

My mother says I get my silliness from *her* mother. Apparently it skipped a generation. She'll enjoy a laugh but she can be stern. My brother and I used to perform for her when we were younger. We would just be as silly as we knew how, standing at the foot of her bed trying to make her laugh. She'd look at us over her glasses and say, "Who took mah chirren? You musta been sweetch at birth. Someone else is raising mah chirren!" She hated when we acted ignorant and didn't speak proper English, so we would do it on purpose. We'd say things like, "Why he had did dat doe?" She'd cringe. We'd howl with laughter.

Surely, trying to pry laughs out of my mom helped in developing my comedy skills. That and my obsessive TV watching. I sat through a shit-ton of *I Love Lucy* reruns growing up, so thank you, Ms. Ball, for your wisdom and influence. I also took note of sitcoms that starred a stand-up comedian—Ellen, Roseanne, Bret Butler, Martin Lawrence, Tim Allen, Drew Carey.

When I was growing up, TV was a mythical thing in a magical land. As much as I felt I was a part of the Huxtable family or that George Jefferson was my uncle, I never thought there'd be a chance of me running into those people. But, as I got older, something shifted in my consciousness and my confidence. Or maybe it was seeing Jerry Seinfeld in my college cafeteria one minute and the next thing I knew that cranky guy talking about his socks was INSIDE my TV set. It may have struck me for the first time that real human beings were on my TV. Being on TV was actually an attainable goal. I could live in that magical land if I wanted to. Anyone could if they were funny enough. I thought I was funny enough. So I said, "Fuck it. Why not me?" And I moved to Hollywood and inside your television.

Chapter Ten

'Tis Better to Give Than to Receive . . . Another FKN Candle

I believe it was Jesus who first said, "It is more blessed to give than to receive." It was probably because he was tired of getting random candles for his birthday every frickin' year. After the hundredth box with that Yankee Candle logo, he was like, "I'm begging you, NO MORE CANDLES. I appreciate the gesture but I'm good. I don't even *like* frankincense. P.S. I'm the son of God. You'd think you'd spring for Voluspa."*

I'm just like Jesus. Well, only in the sense that I don't want your fucking candle. Don't get me wrong, I love gifts . . . that I fancy. I don't fancy candles. And it's not even like I don't like

---

* I know Christ isn't this superficial. I think we can all guess it's me who's over cheap candles. I'm sure Jesus appreciates all gifts presented to him.

candles. I'm just scared of burning my condo down. *And* I have *very* particular tastes when it comes to scents. Nine times out of ten the candle you choose for me will be a swing and a miss. And, as my friend Shameka once told me, I'm not very good at hiding my feelings. So chances are you will see my disappointment in your "thoughtful" gift, your feelings will get hurt, and then I'll feel guilty for hurting your feelings. Then I'll get mad that I hurt your feelings when I know you just randomly grabbed a candle out of a discount bin at Bed Bath & Beyond. My close friends know this about me. I'm tough to please, but I also don't expect or require gifts* from anyone so it works out perfectly.

I swear I'm not the Grinch, I'm just being honest. I'm speaking my truth, people. And the truth is, I LOVE LOVE LOVE Christmas, maybe more than almost anything in the universe. But I much prefer GIVING to receiving.

To understand why, let's go back, deeeeeep into my childhood . . .

Once upon a time, young Marietta couldn't wait to get loads of presents on her favorite holiday of the year. One weekend soon after Thanksgiving ended, Marietta would help her mother replace allll the harvest- and pilgrim-themed household accents with even more Christmas sundry. First, she'd place a giant fake wreath on the front door, then help put up the family's fake tree, which her mom got at a steep discount the day after Christmas a few years before. It was the floor model at Jamesway and had beautiful white branches

---

* This is a stark change from my childhood, which you will see later in this chapter.

and blue ornaments. Come to think of it, it looked more like a tall Hanukkah bush, yet another reason why Marietta's always identified with and appreciated her Jewish friends and neighbors. Oh, how she loved that tree. It matched their living room perfectly, which was very important to a style maven like the Sirleaf matriarch. Fake greenery had always been a part of the family's holiday festivities. This is all that Marietta knew. She had no idea that people actually put real trees in their homes until she visited a friend's home during Christmas break. She'd seen a production of *The Nutcracker* ballet on TV with mention of a real tree but thought it was a construct of the arts. But a real tree in a *real* home? It was very confusing and upsetting to her. Who would want the inside of their home to smell like the *outside*? Doesn't that defeat the purpose of having a house with walls and windows to shut *out* the outside smells?* And the idea of all those needles getting stuck in the carpet was enough to send Marietta into an OCD-induced panic attack.

After trimming the tree with blue-and-white lights and matching ornaments, Marietta helped her mom cover every inch of their house in festive decor as her father's Christmas albums wafted through the house. Some might say it was all a bit much but it was associated with such happiness for her that it didn't matter! A black animatronic Santa stood guard in the foyer with his boo, Mrs. Claus, greeting guests with a robotic dance while judging whether they'd been naughty or

---

* Note the theme of my having particular tastes when it comes to smells. I also don't like the smell of flowers. Love the LOOK of flowers, hate the SMELL of flowers.

nice. Quaint miniature villages and train sets sprinkled with fake snow were displayed on the floor. Harvest-themed towels and dishes were replaced with green-and-red Yuletide towels and dishes. Every tabletop was covered with reindeer figurines and every doorway sprouted a sprig of fake mistletoe. Marietta didn't even get mad when her mother would corner her father under one and smooch him down in a way that embarrasses children whose parents still show each other affection.

No, Marietta didn't mind at all. What did ruffle her feathers was when her mother asked her to light all the electric freakin' candles in every window of their two-story, seven-bedroom house because Marietta was lazy, even way back then. But she sucked it up and did it, because she knew if she was a helpful little elf she'd be handsomely rewarded on Christmas morning with clothes, underwear, games, electronics, and usually a piece of jewelry. It might have all come from Kmart, but Marietta didn't know that and didn't care. All she knew was that she'd be showered with gifts from her loving parents.

On Christmas morning, her mother would ask, "Who gon' play Santa and pass out de gifts?"

We don't care! Marietta silently screamed in her head. *Just give us our stuff!*

Unwrapping the gifts was a magical sensory overload. Imperfectly wrapped presents were torn to shreds with glee, unleashing a bounty of new plastic smells! Mmmmm! Ahhhhh! Every year she'd receive a brand-new Simon game and her father would give her and her mother a special piece of jewelry. Marietta loved and cherished her presents and especially looked forward to that new sparkly treasure she was assured to receive.

So imagine Marietta's shock when one year—the year her family moved into their "new" house in the suburbs—the only gifts she received on Christmas morning were a beige pair of corduroys and a Cabbage Patch doll. A baby doll? Marietta was in ninth grade. Her parents were legitimately tapped out from the move and barely had two nickels to rub together. It was a sobering Christmas at the Sirleafs'. Marietta was so heartbroken but knew her mother would be mortified if she knew how disappointed she was. So she held back her tears as best she could but when she returned to her room, the first room she had had to herself since she was four years old, she cried like a baby . . . an ungrateful, selfish baby.

Ugh. Okay, I'm done with the third person now. . . .

This not-so-very-merry moment was life-changing for me. My mother kept warning me, "We just bought this house. Christmas is going to be light this year." But I had no idea how light she meant. I don't know that I even knew what "light" meant. I thought perhaps only ten gifts each instead of fifteen. I just remember being so devastated, but more than that, it hit me for the first time that some families were even worse off than us. A few years later, the present giving would normalize again at my house, but I got it loud and clear that there were kids out there who got less or nothing—they might be thrilled with a beige pair of pants and OVERJOYED by the sight of a new doll that I'd dismissed as not good enough. I wasn't proud of my behavior, and it wasn't the first time.

Once, my dad, who consistently worked his ass off and

spent his hard-earned money on *things* for me and my family, got matching name rings for me and my mom. Chunky solid rings where our names were written out in script, "Deborah" on hers and my nickname, "Neak," on mine. I was apparently too good for this gift and frowned at what I thought was a "tacky" offering. Debbie wasn't having it and said, "If you don't like it then you won't have it," and took it out of my hand. The funny thing is, *now* I think it's cool in a kitschy kind of way. No matter, Deb has kept a death grip on the ridiculed gift and sometimes she wears both to taunt me. "You *didn't* like it so *you* don't get it."

The lesson I learned *that* Christmas was never look a gift horse in the mouth cuz they will keep that gift and it will haunt you. I think my ungratefulness is what led my family to what I called the "sterilization" of our Christmases after that. It wasn't long after I turned my nose up at the name ring that my family turned to giving gift cards. I mean, gift cards are cool but hardly personal. But the year our Christmas hit rock-bottom was when we all exchanged envelopes of cash. If that doesn't say "I give up" I don't know what does. I blame myself for that. My petulant attitude had brought us to this and I've regretted it ever since.

But I learned something about myself the Year of the Cabbage Patch, which was getting THINGS wasn't what was important. Don't get it twisted, I like things. There are even *some* things that I love (see: ADDICTION chapter). I just don't need people to give me things to be happy. Offer me your time and companionship. Let's spend time laughing and sharing and breaking bread. That's what makes me happy when it comes to the people in my life. I can buy my own things.

Bottom line, don't feel pressure to get me a thing. I don't want you to waste your money or kill yourself to go to Walmart to buy me a sweater that doesn't fit. My reaction is gonna make you feel bad, which will in turn make me feel bad, and now you've spent money to make us both feel like shit. I call this "gift onset guilt." I mean, I'll try my best to fake it, but I'm not Meryl Streep. Yet. So to save us both the awkwardness, just don't buy me anything. I promise it's okay. My cabinets are already chock full o' crap.

I much prefer to play Santa; in that case it's perfectly fine to love the giver if it's ME. Because I don't mean to toot my own horn, but I consider myself a good gift giver.* Ever since that sad Sirleaf Christmas, from that day forward I've made it my goal in life to make sure everyone I know has the best Christmas *ever*. I truly get more joy giving something that people really want without them having to tell me what it is. Even better, I love the idea of getting something someone LOVES. Perhaps it's because I don't want my friends or loved ones to experience gift onset guilt. That means if my mom wants a Kindle to download the Bible App, I'm getting her that Kindle, even though I know there's a 99 percent chance it will sit unused because no one's able to teach her how to work it, like the new Keurig I gave her this year.

I like to play Santa with my sisters-by-choice, too. I've been throwing a Christmas party for my close gal pals for the past fifteen years in LA. In the early days, I'd do a potluck

---

* My heart just sank, thinking what if my friends are reading this and thinking, *Bitch, you* wish *you were a good gift giver.* If y'all are reading this—and you better be reading this, my first book—and think I'm a bad gift giver, please let me down gently.

Christmas party in my studio apartment with eight friends where the only decorations were multicolored lights strung along the ceiling of the bedroom/living room/TV room. Fifteen years later the group has grown to about twelve and I have a considerable amount of holiday décor, which includes a mini *fake* tree, personalized stockings, a mirrored tree for the credenza and, the pièce de résistance, a silver reindeer candelabra. The gift giving was an essential component of my party from the get-go. I'm a huge fan of giving a gift bag.*
Along with the gift bag, I started including a Secret Santa gift, graduated to white elephant, then added additional gift-bag prizes for winning games such as Catch Phrase, Taboo, and Heads Up! Each year I try to do something new that will surprise my friends. Stuffed bears were in regular rotation for a while. I love to personalize gifts, so one year I gave everyone slippers with their names in colored glitter glue. That took more time than I like, so the following year I did personalized pajamas where I had the year and nickname of each friend stitched onto the tops and down the right leg. The pajamas were such a hit, the fête is now officially a pajama party. I love to personalize stuff and people appreciate it.

One year, I threw a makeup-themed party and I had everyone tell me the one product they couldn't live without. Then I bought enough so that everyone got one of each of the favorite products (and I threw in a Plexiglas cosmetics organizer cuz *perf*, duh). Then, because I love a theme, I asked

---

* As much as I love to give a gift bag, I get panic attacks when there's a gift bag at Hollywood events. I used to live to go to gifting suites until I realized most of the "gifts" end up as junk in my guest room closet.

my friend Kimberly Bailey, who owns The Butter End Cakery, to make cookies in the shape of lipsticks, brushes, compacts, nail polish, and hairdryers. And each friend got a personalized cake with the logo of the product they couldn't live without. THAT WAS MY FAVE FAVOR! I just got so excited for my next holiday party!

Okay, so I'm a little out of control, but I don't care. Each year I can't wait to outdo myself. But what I don't like is when I go to all this trouble and somebody doesn't show up. It. Makes. Me. Crazy! And occasionally the next day I'll find one of the white elephant gifts casually left in the lobby of my building. Hardy har har. (You know who you are and I will get you back!)

It's funny. One of my favorite things to do was send out holiday cards. I stopped a few years ago because I didn't "have time." I didn't have time because I sent out over two hundred cards and felt obligated to write a personal message in each. I always thought that the generic

Merry Xmas
—Us!

wasn't exactly "thoughtful" so I committed to making mine personal. Well, it turns out I didn't have the time to sit on my living room floor and write out a personal note followed by "Murry Chrimuh" two hundred times. It was ambitious and proved to be ill-planned because once I did stop, I can't tell you how many people messaged me saying, "I never got your Christmas card!" People live for that shit. But I do NOT anymore, so I just stopped cold turkey. I guess for

Christmas it's more like cold ham. But I had to stop for my own sanity. That's what I get for being a holiday-message snob.

I will, however, *always* have time to plan my annual Christmas party, even though it is a major ordeal, because it's my favorite event of the year. I hate the crowds at the mall but I will suffer through them to make sure all my party gift bags are ready in a timely fashion.* I also need time to wrap my gifts properly without feeling rushed. I'm one of those weirdos who actually looks forward to wrapping dozens of gifts because a symmetrically wrapped package gives me an unnatural satisfaction.

That's the kind of shit I live for during Christmas season. Perfection. Because my friends know me and are all too familiar with my very particular and hard-to-pin-down tastes, they have figured out the best solution to this conundrum of bringing me something without actually bringing me something.

They bring me LIQUOR. Lots of it. They know they can't go wrong with Cîroc Peach, Three Olives Purple (which oddly tastes more like grape than Three Olives Grape) and Disaronno.

I guess all I want for Christmas . . . is booze. It always fits and never goes outta style.

---

* KNOW that I do as much of my shopping as possible online. Only when deliveries will not arrive in a timely fashion do I submit to the torture that is mall holiday shopping.

Chapter Eleven

Ginuwine Isn't Really My Cousin

L ife can change on a dime.
I was killing it on the college circuit, working nonstop, when the worst tragedy in American history went down. September 11. The economy tanked and, along with it, so did my stand-up touring schedule. My bread and butter, my bookings, slowed down dramatically. I had bills to pay. Back in LA, I auditioned for whatever came my way and tried to get into as many rooms as possible with studios, producers, and networks in the hopes of getting another holding deal or a development deal. But the competition was stiff out there. It was hard to stand out in the crowd. It felt like I was being lumped in with one group—funny black female—and the powers that be were making no effort to discern the differences between us. You've heard the phrase, "They all look alike?" Well, apparently, we all WERE alike. I can't tell you how many parts I went out for and lost to Wanda Sykes. Now, I'm funny and Wanda is funny, but we are NOT the same. There were even times when casting directors and producers auditioned actresses, including me,

while they waited to hear if she had accepted their offer. This happens all the time. I am in no way special when it comes to this sort of thing. But when it got really heartbreaking was when I went in to pitch a show to a network and they were like, "What's it about?"

"Well, I'm a judge . . ."

"Um, before you go any further, Wanda Sykes just pitched a show where she's a judge. Sorry."

Gaahhhhd damn! Is this trick gon' take erry job? What are ya gonna do. Wanda was HOT! And everyone wanted her. I don't begrudge anyone their success. I love Wanda, as well as most of the women I've met out on the "African American women who are funny" audition circuit. I'd heard horror stories about actresses trying to sabotage you during auditions. Talking really loud in the waiting room so you can't focus, or trying to intimidate other actresses by walking out of the room and saying things like, "Oof, good luck with that one!" I gotta say, that shit would definitely have worked on me. But I didn't find it to be cutthroat. I think that passive-aggressive behavior is what the average thin white girl going in for the myriad parts available to them goes through. *That* is the struggle of the could-be ingénue. There are so many jobs for them, but still way too many of them.

Black actresses are different. I've found that they are very supportive. When you see them at an audition, they're like, "Hey, girl!" "Kill it." "Do your thing, mamma!" At my very first sitcom audition, Sherri Shepherd was in the room. We'd never met before, and I told her it was my first audition and that I was nervous. She was like, "Don't be nervous. Go in there and do what you want to do. Stick with your choices."

She went in before me and I could hear her in the room. Her read was bold, boisterous, and energetic, and I thought, *That's not what I planned to do.* I immediately started doubting myself and the choices I had made when rehearsing. I went into that room with a completely different agenda, one I had decided on while sitting in that waiting room five minutes after hearing someone else's choices for *their* audition. I went in there trying to be Sherri Shepherd.

For a long time I'd go into auditions thinking, *What do they want?* I'd look at material and try to guess what it was the casting directors might want as opposed to doing what *I* thought was best for the material. It took me a looooong time to make choices about material based on what I thought was best and not worry what "they" had in mind. Because, truth be told, sometimes casting directors, producers, and writers don't know what they want. Sometimes they aren't certain of what they want until you walk in there and give them what they didn't know they wanted. Now when I read a part, I do what I think will be funny or right or poignant. I make my own choices instead of trying to get into the minds of people I've never even met.

Now that I think about it, it might be more of a plus-size blacktress phenomenon. I tended to hear the "good luck" and "break a leg" comments more when it was a room of women of like size. That's not to say that only plus-size gals are friendly or even that there aren't some who might wanna sabotage others, but I do think we've experienced enough negativity that we tend to try to uplift. There's more positive energy in *those* waiting rooms. I at least thought it was real and I learned from it. In the past I'd had moments where I questioned why I didn't get called in for this project or that but have come to an understanding that, just like half shirts and low-rise jeans, everything ain't for *every*body. I trust that there's a reason for everything and don't fall into that "Why not me?" space anymore. I've also taken to forwarding information to other actresses (and actors). If I see something that a friend would be great for, I make sure they know about it and let their reps know to get them in on a project. Why not? It can only bring good karma, right? People have done it for me and I've taken to paying it forward.

When things got really bad for me financially, this sisterhood had my back. I got so desperate for money, I sent out a mass email to everyone I knew in LA asking them to keep me in mind if they heard about any kind of side gig. I was willing to babysit, pet-sit, house-sit. It was an e-version of a WILL WORK FOR FOOD sign. Pride and ego went out the window. I needed to pay my rent. I got one interview to babysit a friend's kid and a response from Aisha Tyler, an old stand-up friend who was hitting her stride in Hollywood and working like crazy.

"I need someone to respond to my fan mail," she wrote. "Do you want to do it?"

I was like, "Hell, yeah. I can sit on my floor watching TV while stuffing envelopes with your headshot. Easy-peasy." So I did that. I got paid to mail out a friend's headshots. I was grateful for it and grateful for my friend. Aisha and I had lunch not too long ago and we laughed about it. I still have some of her damn headshots in my closet. You might ask if it was humbling. It wasn't, because I was doing what I needed until I got to where knew I could be. I never thought seriously about giving up. I mean, in the back of my head, I always thought, *If worse comes to the very fucking worst, I'll pack up my car, drive home to Jersey, and start studying for the MCAT again.* Medical school has always been (and still is, as far as I'm concerned) an option. My father wasn't going to let me starve or live on the street. I always had someplace to go. So because I had that in the back of my mind, I never really feared living in my car. I just really didn't want to have to go to Jersey. That would have been failure to me. Like, "Ugh! If you hit Jersey, your body won't die, but your spirit might." In my heart, I knew I wasn't gonna go home. I always knew something big was coming. I'm one of those people who thinks if you *know* deep inside that something's going to happen for you, it's going to happen. People who are going to be successful know it's gonna happen. And those people tend to hustle until it does happen.

Nothing will deter you from it. Even when it seems like your own agent doesn't care if you're alive. Or should I say "agents"? Let me break down the nightmare of my representation in the early days:

- After I won the Comedy Central stand-up contest, I got a development deal with ABC. I wrote my agent a $12,000 commission check for that deal, and then I can't even recall her sending me out on a single audition for maybe a *year* after that. I politely moved on from her.

- I signed with a new agent at one of "The Big Three" agencies. She was on *Forbes*'s "30 under 30" list of hot agents. Someone had taught me a trick about staying in your agent's mind: Only give them a few headshots at a time, because then you have to keep going into the office to give them new headshots (this was before digital everything). This way you stay in their minds and won't become part of the agency white noise. So I would call every other week to say, "Do you need more headshots?"

1. She was never available when I called.

2. It seemed when she *did* return my call she was always in her car and the phone call would always drop. I know, I know. It's Hollywood. And she's a Hollywood agent. #ParForTheCourse

When I finally got to talk to her, she never needed headshots. "No, we're good," she'd say. Really? You're good? It's been two months and you don't need aaaaany more headshots from me? It was shady but I thought, *I'm with the Big Three!* At least there's *that*, right?

The straw that broke the camel's back was when I got a call from John Papsidera's assistant at the time. John was the first casting director to cast me in a movie. He holds a special place in my heart for his kindness and general badassery. I answered my cell, whose number very few people had because I had JUST gotten it. She said, "Retta! You're a hard person to find!" And I was like, "I am?" She asked if I was still at that Big Three agency. I told her yes and she said, "Oh, because I just called over there to see if you could come in to audition for this pilot John's casting and they don't have you listed as a client." That's what she said. That I wasn't listed as a client. The FUCK? Talk about dropping the ball. I'd have respected them more if they had just dropped me, but to have me thinking I'm being represented and then when potential work *actually* does come through you don't have my name and number on a list?? I was too through. I scheduled my own audition, and as soon as I hung up, I called my manager and asked him to draw up a Notice of Termination. I had zero words for my "hot 30 under 30" agent. That's not true. I had two words: Girl, bye.*

I signed with another agent, who promptly passed me off to a junior agent. I booked a feature film (wut, yay!), shot it, then ran into this kid on the Paramount lot one day. "Ah, Retta," he said, "I gotta visit you on the set!"

"I wrapped that movie a week ago."

The agency dropped me as a client right after that.

Luckily, even during the depths of my misery and frustration with my agency drama, something would happen to keep hope alive. A little appearance here, a little costar there. I had no agent, but between my management and the few people who knew who I was around town, I was able to get the random audition here and there.

Including a little audition for an NBC pilot called *Parks and Recreation*. I remember my manager saying, "It's not anything

---

* When you sign with a big agency, you have no idea who your agent is because they switch you around from agent to agent without telling you. At one point, I didn't know the name of my agent or what he or she looked like. Once, I was at a birthday party at the Formosa Cafe, when a girl came up to me: "Retta? You're so funny, do you have representation?" I was about to talk so much shit about my current agent, then I thought, *Oh my God, this might be my agent. And she doesn't even fucking realize* she *reps me!*

major." I didn't care. I wasn't doin' shit. It's not like producers were knocking down my door begging me to bless them with my thespian magic. I remember seeing Octavia Spencer in the waiting room. It was nice to see a familiar face. There were some other ladies that I recognized but didn't know personally. Octavia got called in before me and then it was my turn.

When I walked in, there were a bunch of people in the room. I don't like when there are a bunch of people in the room. It makes me nervous . . . Who am I kidding? *The room* makes me nervous. Anyway, I did the scene—the character Donna was at her desk in the office reading a book when the new guy in the parks department approaches her and starts chatting her up about the author of her book, who happens to be her fave. The new guy's trying to get on her good side and she ain't buying it. Nothing too challenging, a pretty straightforward scene, A SCENE that wasn't actually in the pilot script. The character had no scripted lines in the pilot but the creators knew eventually she would speak so they wrote this scene so we, the actresses, would have something to audition with . . . as opposed to calling us in to see what we looked like sitting behind a desk. I finished reading the scene with the casting director, which I think went okay, and then just before I was about to leave, the creator/executive producer, Mike Schur, complimented my ToyWatch, which was very popular at the time. I'd just ordered it off a new site, Gilt .com, which was inviting people to become members.

"If you want to be a member, I can invite you!" I said excitedly. Like he wants to be a fucking member of an online shopping site!? But I continued my sales pitch. "Oh my God, you guys, it's normally that price, but I got it for this price. It was almost free, it's so amazing and I love it and I keep getting compliments. I mean, *you* liked it!" I was having a Chatty Cathy mixed with saleswoman-of-the-year moment. I could and *would* have talked them to death if they had let me. I was *that* person.

The other big-deal exec producer, Greg *"The Simpsons* and *The Office"* Daniels looked at me like, "Oh wow, she's a lot." But I think Mike was amused by how enthusiastic I was, how invested I was in this website, and how much I loved this fucking watch.

When I was done, Octavia, who had waited for me, and I walked to our cars together.

"I don't think they're offering much," she said. The part was basically to be glorified background until they figured out what to do with the character.

"Well, I ain't got shit happening." I laughed. "I got nothing going on, I might as well learn what it's like to be on set regularly." I'd done a couple of episodes of sitcoms and one or two TV pilots, but I still didn't feel like I was at home on a set. This would give me an opportunity to watch and learn.

Mike and Greg decided to hire crazy. I got the role of Donna Meagle, office manager for the Pawnee Parks and Recreation Department. There was no dialogue and the first "season" would only be six episodes, but when my manager told me I got the part I was helluh geeked. I don't know if that feeling of elation ever goes away. I still get a flutter and a slight high upon hearing that I booked a part. But you wanna know the best part? I didn't have an agent when I booked *Parks.* For the next seven years, I did not pay that 10 percent to ANYONE. To all my former agents: Y'all played yaselves!

Booking *Parks* was what I'd been working toward for a decade. I had told my parents I was giving up med school to make it in television, and I accomplished that. Plus, it made me feel normal. To wake up every morning and have to go to work made me so proud. I loved being able to say "I can't, I have to work." As a comic, I was usually home during the day. Now, as an actor with a regular gig, when someone would say, "Want to get lunch?" I could say, "Nah, I'm working today." Felt damn good to say that. Like I fit in in Hollywood.

As ecstatic as I was about landing the part, the reality of what I'd gotten myself into started to make me uneasy. I felt like I was in a bit over my head and the odd man out. This was a cast of accomplished improv actors and comics—Amy Poehler, Paul Schneider, Rashida Jones, Aziz Ansari, Nick Offerman, Chris Pratt. Plus, they all seemed to know each other already and they essentially did. They had spent time together once the cast was set. As regulars, they'd done reads and meetings together. I was a costar, so I didn't even meet anyone until the first day of shooting. As improvs, they would play these games on set where they'd name a famous person and you had to do an impression, whether you knew how to do it or not. There were moments where I'd be like, *I don't even know who that actor is, let alone how to do an impression.*

And they were a blue bunch. It was nonstop jokes on set. The filthier the better. I don't work blue. I get too embarrassed. I think people might be surprised by that, but it's true. Were I white they'd have been able to see how much they made me blush. For every scene we had what was called a "Fun Run," which meant after we'd done all of the takes according to the script and all the alts, we'd do one take that was improvised; you could do whatever you wanted. The very first week we had a conference-room scene and Nick ended the scene saying something so off-color that my heart skipped a beat. I was like, *Holy shit, that was ON camera. He's going to get fired!* This was the type of thing they talked about in our mandatory harassment seminar. I quickly found out they were all of like mind. This was how they played. I was quickly on board. I didn't necessarily come up with the jokes but I no longer ran and hid. One of my favorite behind-the-scenes moments was a surprise for Amy provided by Chris Pratt. In the scene, Leslie opens the door to Ann Perkins's house and finds Andy, who, in hopes of winning back Ann's heart after a fight, shows up nekkid. They'd done a few takes where Pratt, of course, wore a merkin to hide his junk but there was one take where Pratt was *merkin-less.* The surprise on Amy's face was fucking priceless, and she has a laugh that you can't help but laugh along with. I enjoyed it to no end. Of course, Pratt received a letter from upstairs saying not cool, you can't do that, bruh.

I think back to these moments and they make me laugh now, but it belies my original insecurities. I'll never forget the first day I shot with Rashida Jones. I knew who she was because . . . Rashida, duh. But I had just found out that she had attended Harvard with our executive producer Mike Schur. I, as you know by now, attended Duke University and Duke has long had an inferiority complex about Harvard. I believe it's because Duke is touted as such a great educational institution but since it's not one of the original Ivies there's been a bit of a chip on the Blue Devil's shoulder. What's crazy about it is that we only feel that way about Harvard. We don't give a shit about Princeton, Yale, or Brown. I think it has something to do with the fact that Duke has been called the Harvard of the South.*

That history in mind, I always wanted to seem like a peer to Rashida. Not that she even knew where I went to school or cared. Why would she? She's got bigger fish to fry. I never brought it up. I just remember the first day we were on set, she said, "Irregardless is in the dictionary," and I go, "No, it's not!" And she's like, "It's used so much they put it in, even though it is not a word." When she walked away, I googled it and wouldn't you know it, she was right. So, at this point, not only am I insecure about my professional background, I feel as though my education isn't on par with those around me. I know it's stupid . . . *now*, but in the moment I thought, *Who am I and what am I doing here?*

Insecurities aside, I loooooved working on the show. I loved knowing and feeling like I was a part of the business. I wanted to work EVERY DAY. I didn't because I was a costar, so I wasn't in every scene or a part of every storyline and because I *wasn't* a regular I wasn't in every episode. Even though half the time I was just sitting at Donna's desk "working" at the computer, I would get so sad when I found out I wasn't in an episode. It made me feel like I wasn't truly a part of the cast. I wanted to be around our cast and our crew. I loved spending my mornings in the trailer with our hair and makeup team. I loved laughing with our camera guys during

---

* There are T-shirts for sale in our campus bookstore that say "Harvard—the Duke of the North."

blocking* rehearsal. I loved singing Shawna Malwae-Tweep†
with Amy, Aziz, and Rashida in the bullpen. I remember being so upset once that I wasn't in an episode that I went on a
last-minute trip to Hawaii with a friend who I was in love
with, but who wasn't in love with me, thinking it would
make me feel better. It didn't. It was a trip he'd planned for a
girlfriend's birthday, but they had gotten into a huge fight
and it was the last time he could use his days in the time-
share . . . blah blah blah. It was a mess and stupid and I don't
recommend that kind of self-soothing.

I didn't feel like the redheaded stepchild forever. The
turning point for me came during season two, filming "The
Hunting Trip." I was helluh nervous because Greg Daniels
was directing and he made me nervous (I now know he's a
sweetheart, but back then . . .). He seemed so serious and was
very quiet. I don't trust quiet people. When I'm comfortable
I'm chatty and I can be boisterous. I used to get in trouble
at school for talking too much. Nothing made me crazier
than people who said I was loud; I fucking hated that shit.
So people who were quiet made me nervous because I always
thought they were judging me. Greg is very quiet and he was
The Man. So I was doubly nervous around him because:

---

* Blocking is when the director and actors go over where the actors will
stand and move to in the scene. The floor is marked with colored tape
on every spot where the actors stop so that the cameras know where
they will be and the director of photography can light each location
properly.

† Shawna Malwae-Tweep was a Pawnee journalist and we used to
substitute her name in for the lyrics of songs we knew. Most popular
was singing Shawna Malwae-Tweep to the tune of the Jackson 5's
"ABC."

1. I thought that he thought I talked too much.

2. He did a lot of takes.

3. The episode required me to run out to my car but I have bad knees and a wonky ankle and the costume department put me in workman boots with a heel. I can't wear ANYTHING with a heel. I was so fucking stressed about how I was gonna manage, it was almost making me sick.

I was freaked but I sucked it up and went up to Greg and said, "Oh my God, Greg, I can't run. I have a bad ankle. I can't run down steps. If the camera follows me, I can maybe do it twice and then I'm done." And he was so cool about it (gasp). I was so relieved that when it came time to cry about my Mercedes being shot, I was so relaxed that I wailed as though grieving the greatest of losses. Greg was dying laughing and nothing could have made me happier in that moment. *Greg Daniels just laughed at something that I did; I will survive this shoot.*

When the episode aired, I remember getting a bunch of tweets about my crying scene. People seemed to enjoy watching me lose my shit over my car being shot. It felt good. It felt like maybe I *can* hang with this crowd.

By the time season 3 came along I started cookin' with gas. Jim O'Heir and I were made regulars on the show. It was so exciting. I remember when Mike announced it to the cast and writing staff at a table read for one of the episodes. I don't think I looked too excited on the outside. I tried to act like it was no big deal, but on the inside I was so happy. *Now* I was in this business. I'd already done close to thirty episodes of the show and was now going to officially be a regular on the show. Oh happy day! So I became a regular and it was great. I mean, nothing really changed that much other than getting a parking spot near my trailer as opposed to having to park in the parking deck.

But, having been on the show for more than a year, I learned some things about myself as an actor. I learned that the character isn't *you*. I used to get upset when I didn't like my wardrobe. Donna considered herself fly and I didn't think her clothes were so fly. It wasn't until our costumer reminded me that Donna lived in Pawnee and these are the options she would have that I came to accept what she wore. *Donna* wears floral prints and endless cardigans. *Retta* does not. I had to think about Kathy Kinney, who played Mimi on *The Drew Carey Show*. She wasn't on the street, wearing that fucked-up makeup and those outrageous clothes. She was playing a part. I was *playing* a part. Being able to separate myself from the part was me maturing as an actor. After a while Donna got to get a li'l more fashionable and when Kirston, our costume designer, let me pick and partially design Donna's wedding dress, I was thrilled.

I have also since learned how to have a thick skin. There was the first time *Entertainment Weekly* shot the cast for the cover of the magazine. And by cast I mean everyone *but* me and Jim. Or the time the ladies of Pawnee did a very glamorous photo shoot for a magazine where there were beautiful gowns to choose from except for the big gal. Nothing fit right and I ended up having to wear a strapless dress and we know how I feel about strapless. Another time, we were doing a promo for the Super Bowl, and the director lined us up to walk toward the camera. Jim and I were on both ends and were going to be cut out. Someone shouted out, "We can't see them!" but the director was like, "Oh, it's fine."

It's in these moments that you find out who really has your back in this business. Turns out, Amy Poehler is the fucking best. She was our mother hen. They always say that the tone of the set is set by the number one. And Amy is just so cool, she's fun, she's funny, she loves funny, she is absolutely not that person who needs to be the funniest. If somebody comes with a funny line, she says, "Say that, say that, say that!" as opposed to those insecure performers who want all the gems all to themselves. You know? She just wants the show to be funny, she wants the work to be good. Then you feel free to try things and not feel like you're going to get knocked down or judged, or if it is funny have somebody be mad that you get to say something funnier. Our cast was not competitive. We only wanted to make the funniest shit possible.

Amy, bless her heart, spoke up for Jim and me several times. "No, it's not fine," she told the promo director. "We need to see everyone, otherwise, what's the point? Why are we shooting this if we can't see everyone?" Basically it got done because Amy put her foot down. (These are clearly first-world problems if you can consider them problems at all.)

The next time *Entertainment Weekly* did a *Parks* cover, they planned to include me and Jim, but only on the inside of the magazine. Once again, Amy came to our rescue. "That's absolutely not an option," I heard she'd said, then she threatened not to do the cover at all if we weren't included. So we got on that damn cover, but Jim's head was completely behind the "ent" in *Entertainment Weekly*.

Because Jim and I became regulars later than everyone else, we really bonded and became work besties. I call Jim my set husband. We shared a double-banger trailer. Whenever there was a food truck at the stages, he would knock on my door. "You want some ice cream? You want a hotdog?" He'd always get snacks for me and then we would sit and talk for hours waiting to shoot our scenes. Jim is like a New York Jewish mom who doesn't have a job because they don't need her to work and she knows everybody's business. Jim would gossip so much, I would just sit in his trailer dying laughing. I was like, "Oh my God, you're like a catty woman!" And he was like, "If you can't say something good about someone, come sit next to me." I loved his crazy ass so much. I used to hate when they were mean to his character, Jerry, because it felt like they were being mean to Jim, and I had to make a conscious effort to be like, *Okay, Retta, it's a character. Fucking relax.* Jim would even say, "Retta, it's Jerry. And it's hilarious."

It took a while for Donna to get her own storylines. My friends and family were like, "When are you gonna have a story?" And I was like, "I don't know, I don't write the show." The truth is, I probably needed time to grow into Donna slowly. I think it was a blessing that I didn't have much to do at the beginning. I was able to watch and learn from the skilled actors, and the more the writers got to know me, the more they wrote to my brand of foolishness. You know what I mean? I really appreciated that she wasn't the stereotypical sassy big black woman in the office. She was a sensible person, grounded, and saw the crazy in those other characters. She didn't have to be the loud person. She got to have her own quirks that weren't stereotypical of what I tended to audition for.

By season 4, episode 4, I was ready for my big episode. It was called "Pawnee Rangers" but it might as well have been called "Treat Yo Self." That's the one that raised my visibility and made Aziz and me a part of pop-culture history. The episode was written by Alan Yang, the Emmy Award–winning cocreator of *Master of None*. When we were filming it, we didn't know it would take on a life of its own.

Our storyline was that Ben was feeling down, so Donna and Tom invited him on their annual "Treat Yo Self Day." We shot the scene where Tom brought the cupcakes and then we shot the talking-head portion:

Tom: "Every year Donna and I treat ourselves. . . . What do we treat ourselves to?"

Donna: "Clothes!"

Tom: "Treat yo self."

Donna: "Fragrances!"

Tom: "Treat yo self."

Donna: "Massages!"

Tom: "Treat yo self."

Donna: "Mimosas!"

Tom: "Treat yo self."

Donna: "Fine leather goods!"

Tom: "Treat yo self."

Donna: "It's the best day of the year."

Both: "The best day of the yeeear."

I remember my friend Britnee happened to be visiting me on set that day. I walked over to her when we were done with the talking head and she said, "That's gonna be huge."

And I go, "What?"

And she goes, "That treat yo self shit, it's going to be fucking huge."

I was like, "Really? Seriously?" I never think anything is funny if I'm doing it.

"Trust me, it's going to be huge."

Sure enough, the night it aired, I had been out. When I got home, I remember checking Twitter and my @ mentions were through the fucking roof. WTF? I was like, what happened? I clicked Mentions and it was:

TREAT YO SELF

TREAT YO SELF

TREAT YO SELF

TREAT YO SELF

TREAT YO SELF

TREAT YO SELF

TREAT YO SELF

TREAT YO SELF

TREAT YO SELF

TREAT YO SELF

TREAT YO SELF

TREAT YO SELF

It was crazy. People were dying. "Oh my god, this is the best!" I couldn't believe how big it got. I used to play a game with my friends where we would go to lunch and I'd bet, "If

Treat Yo Self hasn't been tweeted in the last six or seven minutes, I buy lunch." I never bought lunch. It's still tweeted pretty consistently. Check it. I'll wait . . . It's there, isn't it? Be sure to check the hashtag as well. That counts. People say it all the time. Businesses use it for marketing. There are all kinds of products on Etsy. Target sells Treat Yo Self T-shirts. And now there's even a frozen yogurt shop in Gettysburg, Pennsylvania, called Treat Yo Self.

I once saw someone tweet, "Please stop saying 'treat yo self!' I'm begging you." And I get it. Just imagine how much Aziz and I hear it. There was a point where I thought, *What if I hate this? What if I get to a place where I'm like, "I need everyone to stop saying it."* Here's my thing: People really think that they're the first person to say it to me. Like they are breaking new ground. I'll order food, they'll hand it to me and say, "Treat yo self." I'll be getting on a flight: "Treat yo self." And don't let me post a new purse or a happy-hour cocktail on Instagram. If I don't get a hundred Treat Yo Self comments then something is wrong. I usually try to smile and be friendly about it because for them it's a big deal. They've never seen me before in person and it's likely the first thing that pops to mind. What I don't like is when someone expects me to say it on their Snapchat or in a video to their friend. I'm sorry but I'm not your puppet. I was at a basketball game and this fucking kid came at me, shoving his phone in my face and demanding I say it. And I was like, "I'm gonna need you to back the fuck up off me, homie." And absolutely not. I meeeean, R U D E.

And, just a quick note, Ginuwine is NOT my cousin. I feel the need to point this out because about twice a week someone asks, "Is Ginuwine really your cousin?" Nope. Not my cousin. It was a plot point in a TV show. I don't have a real estate license or own a condo in Seattle or drive a Mercedes. I do, however, love Michael Fassbender and *would* name my Mercedes "Michael Fassbender" . . . if I had one.

I love my *Parks* family. I miss them. Actually I miss the crew most because I don't get to see them often. The cast has a group text and we basically talk every week. We are forever sending pics from when we shot the show and pics from new projects when we get to work with other *Parks* family but mostly we send pics of Aziz sleeping on set. Aziz even sends "sleeping Aziz" pics from the set of *Master of None.**

As an actor, you live in uncertainty. The uncertainty of stability. The uncertainty of longevity. Since I was on *Parks*, a beloved show that made it to seven seasons, people always say, "Oh yeah, you don't have anything to worry about. You'll always work." I don't feel that. I don't trust that. Just cuz I'm known for a pop-culture catchphrase doesn't mean my career is set and I can kick back with my wonky feet up. When *Parks* ended in 2015, it was really sad. But I was ready for the end because it was the only season we knew for sure we were coming back for and that it was to be our last. Every time we did a scene on a particular set for the last time we got sentimental. It was thirteen episodes of good-bye.

I loved that job. I am grateful for that job and the experience it gave me. I am grateful to Mike and Greg for taking a chance on me and giving me the opportunity that jump-

---

* Did y'all know Aziz won an Emmy along with Alan Yang for Best Writing in a Comedy? Woot woot! Go Zizi!! Go Yang!!

started my career. I'm grateful to Amy for showing me what being a gracious class act in this business is and what it means to be a boss bitch. I'm grateful to Aziz for being my TV partner in crime and Jim for being my set hubs and keeping me sane on set. I'm grateful to Nick for taking the lead on all things business when it came to our group and laughing at my foolishness when I didn't think I was that funny. I'm grateful for Pratt's childlike joy for life and for showing me what it is to be a humble superstar. I'm grateful for Aubrey's hidden sweetness, which, if you see it, you know you are loved. I'm grateful for Breezy, Helena, Kirston, JT Fabulous, Liz, Ned, Tom, Johnny, Will, Dustin, Tsang, Lozo, Jeannie, Sara, Morgan, David, Doug, Dean, Gay, Jules, Susie, Steve Day, Terrie, Trim, Aisha, Dave, Megan, Donick, Mande, Levine, Robin, Valeria, Lucchese, Willie, Nathan, Karen, and, most important, Terry from crafty.

I've gotten new jobs since the show ended. I've done several movies and recently was made a regular on Bravo's *Girlfriends' Guide to Divorce*. But I don't take anything for granted. I know there are plenty of actors who have been on a series and when it ends, you never see them again. I don't live in a mind-set that because I was on one show, I'm about to live large for the rest of my life. You always have to hustle. I'm determined to stay above water.

In the meantime, I am embracing "Treat Yo Self" because it will likely be on my tombstone. It's my "Dy-no-mite!" My "Kiss my grits!" My "Norm!" My "Whatchu talkin' bout Willis?" My "Yadda yadda yadda." I'm aight with that. As Donna would say, "That's the Meagle motto!"

Chapter Twelve

Membership Has Its Privileges

The morning after I attended my first-ever Golden Globes, I dragged my ass in to work, hungover like a billionaire playboy post–Victoria's Secret Fashion Show afterparty. I sat at Donna's desk in the Pawnee City Hall bullpen praying for an end to the pain when Hadley, Amy's stand-in, asked, "Good time last night?"

"Oh yeah, it was fun," I mumbled. So tired.

"I heard you met Robert Redford."

"What?" I asked, thinking I'd heard her wrong.

"Robert Redford. I heard you met him last night."

"No, I didn't. Who told you that?"

"Jim," she said. Either she heard him wrong or Jim was clearly fabricating because I for sure had not met Robert. Redford.

After blocking for what felt like an eternity, I had to head upstairs to our cast table read. I was suffering. Had to keep it moving. Needed food. Water. A week for recovery. I slunk into the writer's room and plopped down in my regular chair. I felt a bunch of eyeballs on me.

Everyone else was bright-eyed and bushy-tailed. Hadn't we all been to the same awards show and parties? Why was I the only one doing a Nick Nolte imitation?

"How ya feelin', Retta?" asked Jim with a smile I didn't think was at all friendly.

"I'll give you one guess. Not good." And then I remembered. "You told Hadley I met Robert Redford last night?"

"You don't remember meeting Robert Redford?" he said, almost mad at me.

"Rob . . . ? Nah. I didn't meet Robert Red . . . wait . . . did I meet Robert Redford last night?"

"You drunk bitch!" Jim howled. "Yes!"

A wave of pseudo-memories and legit "oh shit"-ness came flooding over me and woke me from my zombie state faster than an ice-bucket challenge. I kinda remembered meeting Robert Redford last night, but what the fuck did I say to him? Did I embarrass myself? Did I embarrass the show? Did I embarrass NBC?

I'd worked so hard to get to where I was and it had paid off. I was now rubbing elbows with Hollywood royalty! In what alternate universe did I ever think that I would not only attend the Golden Globes, but actually talk to The Sundance Kid, Gatsby . . . *Hubbell*? I'd come a long fuckin' way from watching my favorite stars on my favorite TV shows on the small box in my living room in New Jersey. Being on *Parks* opened up a whole new world to me. It was an admission ticket into the inner sanctum of Hollywood and so many surreal and unexpected experiences that left me scratching my weave, asking, "Did that really just happen?"

I'm not gonna lie, one of the best perks of being on an award-winning, critical darling like *Parks and Recreation* is all the cool shit you get invited to. Some F-list celebs get criticized for showing up to the opening of an envelope, but I'm not gonna judge. Believe me, I get it. It's *helluh fun*. They say never meet your heroes because you'll just be disappointed. But "they" haven't ever seen Emmy winners tipsy on the dance floor. It is a gift from the gods. A gift that for me is ALWAYS perfect.

One of the first things I got invited to after landing *Parks* was the Critics' Choice Television Awards (CCTA). The whole cast was invited and we sat at a table together, which helped me not feel like an imposter/fraud. I had to force myself to keep from staring in this room full of celebs who, for all intents and purposes, were just "hangin' out." I was just "hangin' out" with celebs. *ME*. A girl who used to read *People* from cover to cover. A girl who used to pore over the "Stars—They're Just Like Us" section of *Us Weekly* and think there's no way they're just like me. I'm pretty sure Barbra Streisand doesn't use Krazy Glue and toilet paper to mend a breaking nail—a trick I learned from my mother.

But it's true. Stars *are* just like us, that is the truth. Some need a ton of time in hair and makeup to achieve perfection, and some barely need powder. Some are vegan. Some are allergic to nuts. Some are particular about the octane of gas they put in their cars and some don't give a shit. *I* don't give a shit. I've seen it all. We all have our quirks and idiosyncrasies, so it should be no big deal. Right? Wrong. Because when *Mad Men* star Jon Hamm came over and sat at my table at the CCTAs to chat up Adam Scott, I lost my mind. It was a big fucking deal to me. My God, that is one handsome man in a suit. Jon Hamm is the reason why "tall, dark, and handsome" is a thing. He's the perfect mix of smoldering sex appeal and boyish charm. He's not only good lookin' but has the nerve to have a fucking sense of humor. Come! On! Gimme a fuckin' break here. I'm just a girl on a show trying to act normal in this star-studded room and *this* heavenly body sits at *my* table? I like to think I play it cool, but I couldn't help myself. I tried to sneak a pic of him, as if he wasn't familiar with cell phones and what they can do. *Jon Hamm* was sitting at my table and my friends *needed* to know.

I was just as starstruck the first time I attended the *Essence* Black Women in Hollywood luncheon, if not more so. First of all, it was an honor just to be nominated . . . I mean, invited (I've always wanted to say that!). I mean, holy ever-loving shit, it's like every famous black woman in one room! It was surreal. I felt like the redheaded stepchild in the corner, like, OMG, there goes Oprah, there goes Alfre Woodard, Iyanla Vanzant, Naomi Campbell, Diahann Carroll, Lorraine Toussaint, CCH Pounder, Loretta Divine! Seeing Oprah is not real. I know she's a human being, because she takes on human form, but you can't help but look at her as if you're watching a film. It was fascinating. I didn't even pretend that I might approach her. Everybody was stroking her, telling her, "You're the best! You're so important in my life!" My philosophy was, unless you have something new and interesting to say, just sit back and be glad they invited your simple ass. Because she hears that shit over and over again, and she's been hearing it for a hundred years. Like when somebody comes up to me and says, "Omigod Treat Yo Self!" And in my head I know they are about to tell me how "Me and my best friend have a Treat Yo Self Day every year!!" I know it because everyone tells me the same thing. Almost every person I meet under the age of thirty has told me the same thing. So I get it. Simmer down, I'm not comparing myself to Oprah, I'm just not even gonna fake the funk and swing from her dick because it's all Charlie Brown *waan waan waan waaaan* in her ear. I could tell she was over it.

So I played it extra cool with the Big O, but sometimes I play it so chill, I miss out on some epic shit. One year at Comic Con in San Diego, I was sitting on a low wall in the lounge area at Nobu, waiting for my friends to go into an *Entertainment Weekly* party, when I felt an elbow jab me in my back. I was about to swing around and fuck some shit up when I saw that the elbow belonged to a rather delicious ginger.

"Sorry," I whispered, suddenly coy.

"Don't be, I meant to do that," this fine specimen of a man said in an indistinguishable accent.

Ooooooh, heee hee hee, somebody was tryna be flirty! Okay, I'll play.

"Hi. I'm Michael. What's your name?"

"I feel like I know you," I said with a sense of déjà vu.

"Well I think I know *you*."

"You don't know me."

"What's your name?"

"I'm Retta."

"Say again."

"See? You don't know me."

We made more chitchat. I asked where he was from.

"I'm Irish but I grew up in Germany," he said.

"I live here but I'm from Russia," I joked. Black Russian. Get it? The girl sitting next to him piped in uninvited.

"You are?" she said all doe-eyed.

"No." Silence, cock-blocker!

After about another five minutes my friends signaled they were ready to head to the party. Before I left he smoothly climbed over the wall, gave me a hug and kissed me gently on the cheek. I was like, *Alright, ginger-ginger.*

Halfway through the lobby I had a moment of *holy shit, I think I just met Michael Fassbender.* I turned to my friend to tell her as much and she said nonchalantly, "You know he dates black girls. . . ."

Whaaaaaattttttttttttt?!

How did I not recognize Michael Fassbender?! I was in awe of his massive, enormously wonderful performance in *Shame.* Donna Meagle, my character on *Parks,* named her friggin' car, a gold Mercedes-Benz SUV, Michael Fassbender because "they're both German and they're both sexy as hell." God dammit, there were so many things I could have told him! Such a missed opportunity. I was pissed.

That wasn't the only time I blew it with a famous hottie. Let me tell you a story about how I met Idris Elba. But before I do, let me give some context. By the time I was invited to my very first Emmy Awards, I felt like I *could* belong there. *These are my people, this is my crowd,* I thought. I am someone who walks the red carpet in a dress that was made for me by someone I never met (thank you Rani Zakhem).* I am some-one who Al Roker and Giuliana Rancic wish to converse with, as long as nobody better is within a few feet of me. I am someone who makes friends with the ladies from *Orange Is the New Black* and exchanges digits with Lena Dunham because we bond over the fact that we both have the same fake Chanel iPhone case. I am now asked to take selfies with Laura Carmichael, Lady Edith Crawley from *Downton Abbey*, because she . . . nay, the entire *Downton* cast are my peers. I'm part of this industry.

A part of the industry, but second tier for sure. And no-where does that become more evident than in your party in-vites. Not just what you do and don't get invited to, but what *time*. One of the biggest Emmy parties is called "The Eve-ning Before." The first time I was invited to this soiree was very exciting. My excitement was slightly diminished when I realized I was only invited to attend after 10:00 p.m. The party started at 8:00 p.m. but I wasn't granted entrance until 10:00 p.m. Only A-listers like the Tom Cruises, Jerry Bruck-heimers, and Amy Poehlers of the industry, all of who were on the host committee, and wealthy patrons who donate a ton of money to the event's charity get to go early and mix with the elite of the entertainment industry. Then the riffraff like me come in on the tail end after 10:00 p.m. to pick at the re-mains of the DOZENS of buffet-style stations. All of them served food better than at any wedding I've ever attended.

---

* I was clueless about designer gowns. When I found out I would be going to the Emmys I searched online for dresses. I was thissssssss close to ordering one of those designer knockoffs from one of those scam websites that sends everything in a size 4 in inferior material.

This party has a DJ, games, giveaways, and a particularly posh gift basket presented by Target. So as bootleg as it felt to get the 10:00 p.m. invite, it's still the coolest pre-Emmy party I've ever been to.

All this and I haven't mentioned the myriad stars who go to this thing. The host and executive-host committees are a who's who of Hollywood so you know the guest list is bananas. The first year I went the DJ was Tom Cruise's son, Connor. The line of people looking to meet Tom, who was at the DJ booth supporting his kid, was something out of a Six Flags theme park. You already know I think I'm too cool for school to try to jockey for position at a celebrity's skirt hem, so I chose to avoid the madness. However, this was where I met Idris Elba; tall, dark, sexy British dreamboat Idris Elba. *The Wire*'s Stringer Bell. *Luther*'s Luther. I didn't want to meet him. When people are super-super-hot, I can't look them in the face. It's like looking into the sun. I get weirded out and start thinking and speaking on a third-grade level. I was perfectly content hanging out with *Dexter*'s Jennifer Carpenter and *Parenthood*'s Erika Christensen, who I met that night through my *Parks* pal Ben Schwartz. Many a laugh was had. You also have no idea how much fun it is to watch the famous clown amongst themselves. Martha Plimpton, from *The Real O'Neals*, was my favorite because she's as brassy and bawdy as you'd expect her to be. She was sitting with friends, one of whom was Sophie Monk, and just going HAM on 'em. Straight clowning. I remember thinking she'd prolly kill it on *Wild 'N Out*. It was worth the price of admission (which was free for me and my 10:00 p.m. invite).

Anyway, I was just minding my own bizness, people

watchin' like a muhfuhkuh, when my friend Yvette Nicole Brown said, "I just met Idris, he's really nice. Have you met him yet?" Uh, no, and I don't intend to. She was like, "Come on!" and literally dragged me over to him.

"Idris, this is Retta. Retta, meet Idris."

"Nice to meet you, love," Idris said in that ridiculously charming British accent.

"Hummunahu agiotateerereeaerae bubjabibonbonfbi."

Really? Instead of congratulating him on his *Luther* nomination, or telling him that I'd seen him on that one episode of *Absolutely Fabulous*, or even responding with a "Nice to meet you, too," I could not SPEAK. I stumbled, I stammered. I think I might've gotten out a "Cool." Somebody slap me. Slap me hard.

The next night was the Emmys, which meant Emmy afterparties. As I was leaving the Governors Ball I remember Amy asking if I was going to Fallon's party. I said yeah but I had to stop by one or two other parties beforehand. I remember her saying, "No. Just go to Jimmy's. Don't waste your time." It couldn't have been better advice if it had come from Dr. Phil. Jimmy, who had hosted the awards that night, was having his party at a club on Sunset Boulevard.* Jimmy's

---

* Just so you know, the Emmy show itself is never fun. Jimmy was charming as always, but no amount of charm can make up for how long the show is. The most exciting moment happened in the bathroom when I couldn't get my Spanx back up and the secondary shaper snapped back into position so I just gave up. Oh, and on my way back to my seat I ran into Erika Christensen. I was like, "Hey! So good to see you! Last night was so fun!" She looked at me like I was crazy. "I don't know what you're talking about," she said, all pissy. We hung out at Evening Before, no? "I think you're mixing me up with someone else."

party was off the muhfuhkin chizain. I got to the club with my friend Abbe and we immediately doubled up on champagne. We were early, as were Amy, Tina Fey, and Padma Lakshmi, so we were able to set up shop close to the dance floor. We met some guys who chatted us up and danced with us and were a fun time. Soon the place was PACKED and Questlove had the place J U M P I N G, and trust that I was putting in work on the dance floor. I've got two bad wheels but the right combination of cocktails, atmosphere, and dance hits makes me forget—for the time being—that I will regret that shit in the a.m.

I was in the moment, hardly intimidated by the celestial beings surrounding me. I don't care what crowd I'm in—if the music's good I'm bout it bout it. Jorma Taccone of Lonely Island fame came to my table to hang. With him were his wife, Marielle, and Michael Bolton and Pee-wee Herman. We were all at my table getting our party on. Well, *Abbe and I* were getting our party on. Michael and Pee-wee were taking it all in. If anyone had ever told me that one day I would be sharing the same groove space with Michael Bolton, Pee-wee Herman, and one-third of Lonely Island I'd have told 'em they should go sleep it off cuz . . . drunk.

At some point I ended up in the middle of the dance floor

At first I was like, was she that drunk? How could she not remember? Meanwhile, I'm the dumbass. Because it wasn't Erika Christensen at all but Julia Stiles. Apparently this happens to her all the time. But you know what? I don't even feel half bad about it cuz people do this to black folks all the time! I get confused with Yvette Nicole Brown, Loni Love, Sherri Shepherd, Octavia Spencer, Danielle Brooks, and Gabourey Sidibe. All these women are wonderful. I love them. I'm *not* them.

with Taye Diggs and next to Julianna Margulies, star of my fave show *The Good Wife*. I was double-fisting champagne and she was single-fisting her Emmy statue for Best Actress in a Drama.

"You did that shit!" I yelled to her over the music.

"Yeah, girl!" she yelled back.

I'd never met her in my life, but I had a moment with Alicia Florrick.

The next morning, Rashida, Rob, Jim, and I had an obscenely early call time on the set of *Parks*. I gingerly made my way to work, certain I smelled of day-old alcohol on three hours of sleep.* I couldn't have looked or felt worse. Once again, a bunch of eyes were on me, including the baby blues belonging to Mr. Rob Lowe.

"Heard about you and Taye Diggs," Rob smirked.

WTF? He wasn't even *at* the party! Jimmmmmm!

That was one of the most fun nights I'd had in my fourteen years in LA. I've attended the Emmys two more times since then, and each time is better than the last. The best part is I now get invited to the parties without having to sit through the awards show. Trust me, it's ideal. I got to the party early with my friend Sandi McCree, who played Delonda Brice on *The Wire*, and we got a first-class seat at the bar. Two guys came up, ordered drinks, then started talking to Sandi. If you know Sandi, you know she can hold court with just about anyone. And she's the type to call everyone "baby" and "sweetheart."

_____

* There was so much more to go down that night but I will refrain from elaborating to protect the innocent. There was an incident of motorboating. *That* I can tell you.

"Where do I know you from?" asked the young guy, who had a British accent.

"I don't know if you know me, I've only been in a couple of things," Sandi answered. "I was on *The Wire*?"

"Shoot oop!" he marveled, his eyes wide and lit up like a pinball machine. "Can't believe that's you! I loove *The Wire*! It's the only American telly I've watched in a bit. You're so good!"*

Sandi was kinda feeling herself. This darling English boy (he was too young for either of us) was showering her with praise. When he walked away, Sandi, who wouldn't recognize herself in a mirror, turned to me and said, "I recognize him, what is he from?"

"Oh, you recognize Robert Pattinson? Is that right? You RECOGNIZE him?" She's the fucking worst. And the FUCKING best. You gotta love Sandi. She's ride-or-die . . . and often clueless.

Later on, after we'd been drinking for a while, we headed out to the patio, because much of the party had moved out there. On the way out, the hallway got bottlenecked and I was pinned against the bar. Suddenly, out of nowhere, Jon Hamm swooped in.

"RETTTTTTTTAAAAAAAAAAAA!" he bellowed like Marlon Brando in *A Streetcar Named Desire*. Kisses me on the cheek, kisses me on the other cheek, kisses me on the other cheek, kisses me on the cheek, kisses me on the other cheek.

---

* Please forgive my poor attempt at writing a British accent. I can't *do* one, much less write one.

    a. He knows my name.

    b. He thinks he knows me enough to be kissing me on the cheek.

"Heyyyyyy, Jon Hammmmmm," I whispered.

"You having a good time?" he asked rhetorically and kept it moving.

I was legit stunned, like a zombie. Sandi came up.

"WTF is up with you and Jon Hamm?"

"It happened, right? It was real!" I was stunned.

1. Because I had just had a surreal Jon Hamm moment.

2. Because Sandi knew who the fuck he was. And I *needed* her to say that to me, otherwise I'd have gone through life thinking it was a waking dream. I rode that high and told that story for a full year. I even told it onstage once at a college and they put it in the school newspaper. I got a Google alert about it and immediately panicked. What if he saw it and thought I was lame for telling that story . . . onstage, no less? I felt a little bit crazy about it. But Jon obviously never saw it. Even better, the next year, he did the *same* thing. He and Amy hosted a "Loser's Lounge" party at Soho House. They'd both been nominated several years in a row and, having not won, decided to celebrate that fact. Anyone who showed up with a statue, like Tina Fey and Ty Burrell, had to donate $1,000 to the Worldwide Orphans organization and check their award at the door. You couldn't bring that shit into the party. P.S. The guest list was anything but losers.

I was sitting on some low-ass chair and Jon Hamm came up, screamed "Rettttaaaaaa!" and yanked me up out of the chair onto the dance floor. It was early, so the dance floor was empty and I was so stressed dancing with Jon Hamm, I almost couldn't take it. Not just because I have raggedy-ass knees and was terrified they would buckle and leave me facedown on the dance floor, but because I'd have been facedown on the floor in front of Jon freaking Hamm! He started chatting with me and I almost said, "I'm gonna need you to back the fuck off, Jon Hamm, my heart can't take it. Stop talking to me. Do you know who you *are*? Jon? Hamm?"*

But I played it cool with him and *Vampire Diaries* creator Julie Plec (I feel like I've been her nightmare ever since meeting her, I'm obsessed with that show) and most of all Shonda Rhimes, who knew me from my live-tweeting *Scandal*. She told me I was funny and I might have gone home and journaled about it. *Might*. I took the compliment graciously on the outside, but inside my head I was screaming, "ARE YOU FUCKING KIDDING ME! That is the woman responsible for MerDer." It was a legit moment for me.

The Emmys are cool but they don't hold a candle to the Golden Globes, which I've been to once. It was the second time Amy and Tina hosted. The reason they are more exciting than the Emmys, for me, is because there are television AND film stars. And maybe even more important, There. Is. Alcohol. BUT, and this is a big BUT, let me tell you what happened to me on the red carpet. My publicist, Tej, announced me to the gallery. The first photographer on the line looked

---

* I don't know what it is but I always have to say Jon AND Hamm when talking about Jon Hamm. My friend Rosa laughed at me once when I referred to him as Jon. It just sounded too familiar. Like, ooh oooooh, look at you. What, are you *friends* with Jon Hamm all of a sudden?

at me, put her camera down, and said, "I'm good." She didn't want to take my picture. When some of the other photogs recognized me and yelled, "Retta! Retta!" to get me to look their way, only then did that photographer aim her lens up at me.

I held my finger up at her and said, "Nuh-no, you're *good*." I was so fucking pissed. Really, bitch? I HEARD you. All you had to do is hold up your camera and pretend to take my pic. And who was it gonna hurt if you DID take my pic? If you need to save the room on your memory card you could erase that shit as soon as I take a step down. Then you wonder why actors have substance-abuse problems. That kind of humiliation can drive a girl to drink. Which this girl did. Moët happened to be a Golden Globes sponsor and as soon as I finished the carpet, I saw a promo girl carrying a tray with mini-bottles of the bubbly.

"Want one?" my publicist asked.

"No. I want two!" I was hot, thirsty, and feeling vulnerable. I took 'em to the head like water. I wasn't worried, I knew the Golden Globes served dinner. Rashida had gotten to the end of the carpet by this time, so we started talking. Then when I got inside the banquet room, I ran into Lena Dunham. I chatted with her for a bit until Jennifer Lawrence walked up.

"Do you know my friend Jen?" Lena asked.

"Why no, I do not know your friend *Jen*," I said, as if it was the most normal thing in the world. "Hi, *Jen*. I'm Retta." I said it like we were peers and I tried to mean it!

As I turned to look for my table I saw Josh Charles. Josh and I had become friends on Twitter. I was live-tweeting *The*

Good Wife, and he tweeted me to say he found me amusing. (I've made a handful of friends on Twitter. It's like my non-sexual Tinder.) We were meeting for the first time and had a nice chat in person. By the time I got to the *Parks* table, dinner was being cleared. The hell? How's that possible? Well, apparently, they serve dinner *before* the show so as not to have too much activity *during* the show. All that was left on the table was a basket of bread and a magnum of Moët so giant I thought it was fake. It wasn't. I couldn't even lift the bottle, so gentleman Jim poured me a glass of champagne. And I believe he was filling it up every time mamma got low. I don't know. What I do know, what we all know from the very beginning of this chapter, is that I got fucking TRASHED.

Before the show, many a famous person came up to our table to talk to Rashida, who is like the female version of Six Degrees of Kevin Bacon. RaRa knows errybody. Drew Barrymore, Ryan Phillippe, even Dame Helen Mirren all popped by our table to pay their respects. "I'd love to do your show!" Helen told us all. I believe my response was, "Shut your freaking face, Queen!" An elegant homage to her stunning portrayal of Queen Elizabeth, wouldn't you say?

About a quarter of the way into the show, I was hammered and I had to pee. The bathroom was right next to our table, which was gross but also exciting because everyone had to pass by our table to go tinkle. This included Emma Thompson, Jared Leto, and Leonardo DiCaprio. When I got there, there was a freaking huge line. It took forever and I was legit seeing double. Finally, I'm next and suddenly I see Taylor Swift, who's been behind me the whole damn time, walk past me to go to the stall.

"Taylor!"

"What? Oh, were you next?"

"Yeah, bitch, we been standing in line *together* for the last ten minutes!" And I sashayed past her and went to the open stall. Now, here's the rub. I was so drunk I didn't realize I went to the bathroom during Amy's category, Best Actress in a Comedy/Musical and whatever else is in that category's title. But I'm thinkin' Taylor Swift did it on purpose (of course I'm making this up—I have no proof) cuz the year before, Amy and Tina made that crack about her staying away from Michael J. Fox's kid, who had been a Mr. Golden Globe. But Taylor didn't think that was funny and, in a *Vanity Fair* interview, she spit out Madeleine Albright's famous quote, "There's a special place in hell for women who don't help each other." I found this most curious because if you really want to help a woman out, you DEFINITELY don't cut her in line for the bathroom at the Globes. That's *gotta* be in the Girl Code, no? But as I said, I've got no proof of any of this. I'm just sayin'. When I walked back out to the table, everybody was like, "Amy won!" I was so pissed I missed it, and there's a very sweaty picture of me somewhere on Glamour.com that captured this very moment.

I didn't realize it at the time, but I blacked out at some point at the table. After the show, everybody was milling around and leaving, and I had gotten up, sat in Sophia Vergara's seat and turned my chair around to face our table. I had my feet out because I'm classy like that. This older man walked by and stepped on my foot and I was like, "Owwwww!"

Turns out it was Robert Redford.

I was like, "Bruh, you just stepped on my foot!"

"I'm so sorry," he said.

"It's all good, homie."

Yeah, I said that, or something close to that, to Robert Redford. But here's why Robbie Red is cool as shit—he didn't judge my drunk ass. I'm sure he's seen it all. As a matter of fact, he found me amusing and stopped to chat.

"You like the show, Bobby? The girls did their thang."

"Amy and Tina were great!"

Now, who should be watching this tomfoolery go down but Idris Elba! Intrigued by how animated I was with Robert Redford, he came over to get in on the party. "What's going on here?" he asked.

"Oh, just having a bit of a chat with Robert here," I slurred. "Sometimes he steps on your foot, you know. Hollywood legends can do that."

I wish I could tell you what else we all talked about. I cannot. I only know what my costars saw and threw in my face the next morning. There is one more gem of information from that night that I have zero memory of but was happily reminded of by my executive producer Mike Schur. Schur told the table the best part of the night was when Michael Fassbender walked right up to me and said hello. As he walked past our table I turned with a sly smile and announced to the table . . .

"He likes black chicks."

You guys, I nearly died. The HELL was I doing?? The only thing I can assume happened was that he must've been headed to the bathroom and in my drunken haze I likely stared at him with such focus that he felt compelled to say hi. Instead of basking in the beauty and wonder that is Mr. Fassbender,

I felt obliged to share the single piece of information that I knew about him.

I'm not particularly proud of my actions, but I am delighted to have such colorful if not urbane tales to share with you all.

My first head shot. Nowhere
CLOSE to being the shit . . .
but on my way!

My prized personalized Kings jersey given to me by Pat Donahue, director of LA Kings social media, aka "The Man Behind the Tweets."

My first time watching a game seven rows from the glass. Not having glass-banging access stressed me out.

Noel Vasquez

GO KINGS GOOOOO!!!!

Noel Vasquez

That is when I knew just screaming wasn't enough. I had to get in the game if I was to ensure this win. I was gonna make this shit happen! Red Blazer had a different idea:

"Ma'am, what do you think you're doing?"

"I have to bang on the glass."

"Ma'am. Please return to your seat."

Noel Vasquez

"But it's just so exciting."

"Please return to your seat, ma'am."

I eventually took to just leaning on the glass. It worked. We beat the Blackhawks 5-2 that night.

Me in the commissioner's box with Jay Ferguson and the luckiest kid in LA at the time. His first hockey game was during playoffs in the commissioner's box.

Me with Uncle Gary, aka Gary Bettman, NHL Commisioner.

It was a good day.

My excitement to see Hamilton *for the first time.*

On my way to the Richard Rogers Theater for the last preview before opening night with my bestie Rosa and her cousin Francesca.

My Hamilton *playbill.*

The Hamilton *stage.*

Can you see the excitement?

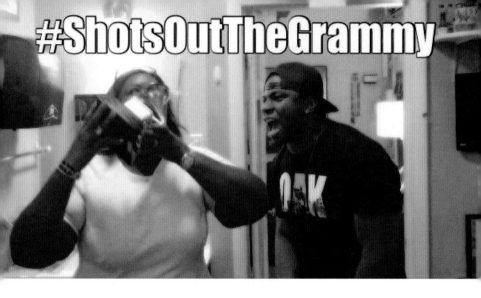

After seeing the show for the fourth time, which was Lin, Leslie Odom Jr., and Philipa Soo's last show, I was able to participate in the now-famous post-show ritual started by Daveed Diggs, #ShotsOutTheGrammy!

Chapter Thirteen

I Would Puck Witchu

If you follow me on social media, you may know that I am a Los Angeles Kings fan. I'm not kuh-ray-zee, but I am definitely enthusiastic. I love me some Kaaannnngggsss. I know that meeting a black woman with a love for hockey is a bit like stumbling upon a unicorn in the woods . . . or a unicorn anywhere. I'm sure it'd be just as surreal finding a unicorn in downtown Chicago. But here I am.

So how does a black girl from Jersey become a hockey fan?

I was on Twitter one night reading my @ mentions when I saw a tweet from the LA Kings account inviting me to come to a game:

@LAKings: @unfoRETTAble how could we persuade you to come to a LA hockey game and live tweet it?

@unfoRETTAble: .@LAKings Hahaha. I'd love to but I don't know jack a/b hockey. I'd just talk about who was cute on the sideline. #IsThereEvenASideline

---

@LAKings: @unfoRETTAble that would be absolutely perfect. We have some good lookin gents on the team. @rainnwilson knows.

@unfoRETTAble: .@LAKings Done. P. S. Congrats on that shiny cup y'all won. It's real purty.

@LAKings: @unfoRETTAble amazing. DM us and we'll get you all hooked up. and thank you very much, you should see the rings.

@katieferg: @LAKings @unfoRETTAble Holy. Crap. So jealous! Retta is absolutely the greatest person on Twitter. Have fun!

@LAKings: @katieferg she's a legend!

That last one was just so y'all would know I AM LEGEND.

I decided to go, and took my friend Ted with me to the game because I didn't know shit about hockey. He's a big sports fan, so I figured he'd be interested in this version of "lacrosse on ice." We had the VIP hookup, which means we had free valet parking. And while valet parking at the Staples Center for Kings games is wayyyyy cheaper than, say, for a Lakers game, free is free. It made me feel fancy.

When we got there, we were greeted by Pat, a handsome, bearded young man who is the director of digital media for the LA Kings, aka the guy behind the tweets. He was with Heather, a delightfully sunny blonde. They introduced them-

selves, and then Pat handed me an official jersey that read
TREAT YO SELF on the back. Pat was a big *Parks and Rec* fan,
followed me on Twitter, and thought I was funny and "legendary" at the live-tweet, which is what led to the now-
monumental invite. He had had the jersey *made* for me. For
ME. A total stranger had gifted me a personalized piece of
clothing. I mean, the free parking was already enough to
make the trip worth it, but now this? Needless to say, I was
helluh geeked. I basically made this trip for the beer and
ended up with a new article of clothing! The Kings coulda
been the worst team in the league, but that simple gift opened
my heart to these yet-unseen ice Vikings.

(That jersey is now one of my prized possessions. Pat
would later say in a radio interview that getting me to become
a Kings fan is one of his proudest moments. And I told him
it was the jersey, homie. It. Was. The. Jersey.)

Once we got inside, Heather took us down one level and
through some heavy double doors that were manned by a security guy who was very serious about checking that our tickets allowed us on this level. The hallway was lined with
photos of LA sports stars and championship teams including
Kobe, Shaq, and the National Championship–winning Lakers. I was like, "Daaaaaang. Okaaaay. I can hang with this
crew." Then we entered another hallway that looked like it
could serve as the passageway for deliveries, i.e., it was *not*
pretty, so I was wondering, *Where the hell is this chick taking
us?* As if reading my mind, she told us: "We're going to the
Chairman's Room." Not gonna lie, my posture straightened
a little, and I strode as though newly knighted. Your girl was
doin' big thangs.

The Chairman's Room* turned out to be a li'l barroom that had snacks and TVs playing sports channels. I assumed the bar served free drinks and was geeked about the prospect of a comped buzz (I believe I mentioned my pleasure in free gets—see "valet" above) but alas, it was a full-compensation bar. There was an older black couple at the bar, and for me it wasn't a big deal cuz this is LA. Black folks are everywhere, right? But the novelty was lost on me because I forgot *where* I was. I was at a hockey game, in the Chairman's Room, where people with the baller-baller/shot-caller tickets hang out. The novelty was not lost on the older gentleman, who, upon see-ing me, lit up with such excitement that I thought maybe I knew him. I didn't. He was like, "Hey, sistuh!" A little thrown by his eagerness, I was like, "Heyyyy . . . sir." And then it dawned on me. We were THREE unicorns in a basement bar. Even this unicorn couldn't believe it.

When it was time for "tip-off" (that's what I called it cuz, as I mentioned, I didn't know shit about hockey), we left the Chairman's Room. Heather directed us toward a group of people gathering near a tunnel, and that's when I saw them. THE PLAYERS. They were click-clacking right toward us. They were fucking UGE. I say UGE because a friend of mine says UGE when she finds things are even bigger than HUGE. I had no idea they were so tall, so massive. They looked like the Chi-

---

* I spend a good deal of time in the Chairman's Room in between periods and after the games, especially when we win. And there's a fun game I stumbled upon while there. I take selfies with my friends and then AirDrop them to any iPhone that shows up on my phone. It makes for many a laugh because you watch as people slowly look around trying to find the culprit who has invaded their personal cell phone space. It's fun. You should try it.

cago Bears defensive line if they wore lifts in their cleats. Just enormous. THIS piqued my interest. Nothing makes a big gal like myself feel petite and feminine like a pack of giants striding by on the way to a brawl—literally. Hockey is basically a melee on skates with a few goals here and there. I like to call it the Clash of the Ice Titans.

We had second-row seats and were next to Colin Hanks and a friend of his. Colin and I had recently met at a staged reading, so it felt as though I had a crew. I placed my beer in the cup holder and opened the program to see what these titans looked like without helmets. I was pleasantly surprised to find that more than one of them was hot like fish grease. Coupled with how large they were, this made me feel warm things inside. I promptly pulled out my phone and created my first hockey Vine vid-tweet, called "They Can Get It."

Both Colin and Ted tried to explain the game to me, but they might as well have been speaking Swahili for as much as I understood. I did, however, make an analogy that Colin was impressed with: "icing" is to hockey what intentional grounding is to football. He said, "I can't believe I've never thought to make that comparison," and I thought I was a sporting genius. But that was as far as my genius went. To this day, I don't get how the players know exactly when to substitute from the bench without so much as a hand gesture.

I was having such a good time that even Bailey the Lion had me in stitches, which is quite a feat, seeing as mascots freak me the frack out. By the end of the second period, we were down 2-1, but no matter. I was in hog heaven because I had a cold Newcastle and live, thrilling, action-packed entertainment.

My bubble was burst when Ted told me that if the Kings lost the game, I would be considered bad juju and would likely not be invited back. I panicked as though I were about to miss the last flight home for Christmas. That third period started, and I'd never cheered so hard for something I didn't understand in my LIFE. We scored two goals that period and won that game. I looked at my Twitter feed at the end, and there were tweets regaling me as good luck! I reveled in the honor as though I had actually had anything to do with the night's win.

> **@mabrywilliams:** Okay so clearly @unfoRETTAble is a good luck charm and has to go to every game now!
>
> @LAKings make this happen!

> **@OffTrackCooking:** @unfoRETTAble I gotta say you brought some good ass luck down there! Nice job! You ever need a game-mate let me know!

> **@unfoRETTAble:** @OffTrackCooking haHA!!! I does what I does.

> **@ColinHanks:** Sat next to @unfoRETTAble during her first hockey game. She brought the @LAKings good fortune.

> **@chanelleberlin:** My phone died at the very end, but what a HUGE win for the @LAKings. Tadah forever!

> @unfoRETTAble, congrats on being good luck.

> @unfoRETTAble: @chanelleberlin Haha! Thanks!

> @Jonathan_Biles: Good luck charm like
> @unfoRETTAble. MT@BillSimmons: Went to
> Blues-Kings. My daughter is 12-1 lifetime in
> playoffs.

After that, I was hooked. I attended several games the following season. I would always bring my jersey and put it on once I got there, because I didn't want to do anything different from my last "good luck" effort. Because I attended games as a guest of the organization, I was given prime seats. A few times I sat in the owner's box, but more often than not, I was seated on the glass near the team, and *that* was my favorite. I was ALL IN. I was a superstitious, jersey-wearing, glass-banging, full-fledged Kings fan.

I was often reunited with my homie Colin Hanks at the glass and he gave me a few tips on sitting on the glass:

1. Never eat during the game because you WILL be photographed stuffing your face. Nothing like seeing a pic of yourself on the internet with a hotdog shoved down your gullet.

2. Never sit your beer on the ledge because skaters moving at full speed WILL slam up against that glass and that beer WILL become one with your lap.

I had been so accustomed to sitting on the glass that the one time I was seated in the sixth or seventh row behind the

Blackhawks I felt like the redheaded stepchild. I know, I know, high-class problems. Trust me, Heather, who got me the seats, let me know I was in NO WAY a redheaded stepchild in the seventh row during game 5 of the Blackhawk series. We actually had a ball because we were seated next to some guys who were not only hilarious but gentlemen, to boot, cuz they bought us beers. Again, I like beer. Anyway, because I had become superstitious at this point, whenever the Kings scored I needed to bang on the glass . . . otherwise we wouldn't win . . . obvi. *So* when we scored our first goal in that game, I ran down to the glass to bang on it and was promptly stopped by security. What I didn't realize, because I was always seated on the glass near the team, was that the glass behind the teams was ACTUAL GLASS, not Plexi. Dude was tryna keep me from causing some real prahlums.

I also hadn't realized that the photographers on the other side of the ice were capturing the whole thing. The Breakdown:

A Kings fan watches her team intently.

Yes! Goal! Go Kings Go!

GO KINGS GOOOOO!!!!

That is when I knew just screaming wasn't enough. I had to get in the game if I was to ensure this win. I was gonna make this shit happen! Red Blazer had a different idea.

"Ma'am, what do you think you're doing?"

"I have to bang on the glass."

"Ma'am. Please return to your seat."

"But it's just so exciting."

"Please return to your seat, ma'am."

I eventually took to just leaning on the glass.

It worked. We beat the Blackhawks 5-2 that night.

At this point I was clearly ALL IN . . . almost. I was 100 percent behind the Kings. I DID BELIEVE, but I started getting tweets from other Kings fans to put Justin Williams on my lock screen. Apparently this was becoming a thing, a thing I just wasn't into. I mean I'm superstitious, Justin is my boo and Mr. Game 7, but really? I just wasn't feelin' it.

So it's game 7 of the semifinal series and we're playing in Chicago. The game does *not* start off well. Less than halfway through the first period the Blackhawks went up 2-0. I was at a bar called The Belmont in LA with some friends watching the game. Inside, the place was packed with Blackhawks fans who were out of their minds with glee. *I* was sick to my stomach. It was crazy. It looked like they were about to blow us out of the water. I kept getting these #JustinWilliamsLock Screen tweets and was getting annoyed that people had nothing better to do than harass me about this stupid lock screen. Let's put our energies into willing a Kings goal, for God's sake. Eight minutes later we scored a goal that had to be reviewed and I took that time to look through my @mentions. People were insistent about this lock screen and I thought to myself, *This game is going to be kuh-ray-zee.* Fuckin' 'ell, what could it hurt? I googled pics of Justin, found one that I thought he looked supes cute in, and I swear to God just as I hit SET LOCK SCREEN do you know that motherfucker scored a goal to tie it up?!?!?! I. Lost. My. MINNNNNNDDD! I was like, HOLY SHIT, that shit worked? My heart was racing. I finally recovered and calmed the hell down to go back to watching the game only to have Chicago score within minutes to take back the lead 3-2.

The second period starts and not much is happening. It's a full ten minutes and I'm anxious so I start rubbing the lock screen for luck and I shit you not, we scored AGAIN!!!! It was 3-3 and I'm thinkin' this lock-screen nonsense is legit. Of course I am now maniacal about it. I'm rubbing that iPhone screen like there's a genie locked inside. We end up going into overtime, again, and winning the game 5-4 off of a random goal that bounced off a Blackhawk's shoulder. That goalie didn't have a chance, and I'm not gonna lie, I really started to feel like I might actually be good luck. No sooner did the game end than the tweets from Rangers fans started coming in. All of them warning me how they were gonna kick our asses. I was like, can a bitch get a second to enjoy this win?? Shit.

Next up was the final series against the New York Rangers. I knew tickets were going to be impossible so I didn't bother asking, and not because I thought I'd be told no but because I didn't want anyone to think I was stupid enough to think there would be Stanley Cup tickets available. I can't remember what I was doing, but I received a text from mah girrr Heather:

> **Heather:** Retta!!
>
> **Heather:** 2 things:
>
> **Heather:** Are you around Saturday if I can get you tickets? It's brutal, but I will fight for them
>
> **Heather:** Also, the NHL is interested in talking to you about presenting at the NHL awards in Vegas. If you are, what is the best way for them to reach out?

Whaaaaa? Am I avail to come to a Stanley Cup championship game?? Yaaaasssssssss. I was so geeked because, as much fun as I had during regular season games, Staples was gonna be off the motherfuckin' HOOK for this shit. And then, as if THAT wasn't enough, I received this:

> **Heather:** So the commissioner of the NHL would like to host you in his box. Will be fun—he hosts a lot of high profile types like yourself
>
> **Heather:** I will put tix at valet for you boo. Woot Woot!!
>
> **Me:** For reals??
>
> **Me:** Can I bring someone?
>
> **Heather:** Yep yep—to both
>
> **Me:** Hahahaha. Cool.
>
> **Heather:** I will come see you—this is so GD stressful/exciting!!!!

Hol' up ! Hol' up! Hol' up! You mean to tell me I'm 'bout to hang wit da commish? Girrrrrrl you ain't said nuttin' but a word.

So I go to Game 2 of the Kings/Rangers series at Staples Center. The commissioner's box is one of those baller-baller suites with free eats and beer. It's a couple doors down from Hyde Lounge, which is a straight-up club right there in the stadium. For reals. An *untz untz untz* club IN the arena. There were some important-looking folks in the box and some familiar faces, including Will Arnett and his son Archie, whom I have met on several occasions on the set of *Parks And Rec*, Chloë Grace Moretz and her brother Ethan, and Jason Reitman. I gave a quick hello to Will and Archie, then my friend Gina and I sat in the front row, and who is already there? None other than my homie Colin Hanks. He and his wife, Samantha, were there to root for our Kings and it was a full-circle moment for me. Jay Ferguson and his son came not long after we sat down and sat next to us. Jay's son was probably around eight years old and this was his first game. His FIRST GAME! And he's at a Stanley Cup finals game in the commissioner's box.

And I thought *I* had been livin' high on the hog. I soon meet Nirva Milord, director of entertainment publicity and corporate communications for the NHL, and she introduces me to Gary Bettman, the commissioner of the NHL. Soooo you could say I was rubbin' shoulders. My first Stanley Cup series and I'm chillin' wit da commish. No big. Relax.

The game was exciting for no other reason than #Because ItsTheCup. The Rangers scored two goals in the first period and I was just sick, but then I had a moment of clarity. We had been doing this ALL post-season long. I was talking with one of the important-looking people in the box and she said the same thing. The Kings weren't happy unless they were coming from behind. Once I had made my peace with this notion, I could actually calm down. Then Nirva comes up and asks if I would do an on-camera interview for the championship DVD. I said sure, but I was nervous because as much as I had grown to love the Kings, I still didn't know *SHIT* about hockey.

I go into the hallway to do the interview, and I take my

friend Gina with me to be on grooming duty. She was to watch me and help mitigate the shine on my face because, after Whitney Houston, no one sweats on camera more than me. They ask me a few softball questions that I answer simply enough, but then they ask something along the lines of how do I feel about this matchup and my answer was as follows:

"I don't know much about hockey or the Rangers but here's what I do know. The Rangers are helluh fast on that ice and they have the hottest goalie in the league but FUCK the Rangers!"

What the hell?? Who exactly did I think I was? I JUST became a Kings fan and now I'm talkin' shit? Oof. Clearly I was trippin'. All I could think was *please don't put that nonsense on the DVD* . . . ESPECIALLY if the Rangers win. That would NOT be a good look.

I went back into the suite to watch the second period and we scored. Our crowd went F'n apeshit. We were *in* this thang. But it didn't take long for the Rangers to score. They led 3-1 and once again we were like, WTF? I was now starting to regret my bravado in that interview. Then they scored AGAIN and it was like *well, fuck.* There's no stopping these dudes. And then in the third we scored two goals, tied that shit up, and it was on like Donkey Kong. We were so geeked we didn't know WHAT to do. I'd had so many beers and peed so many times that I'd burned a track in the carpet from my seat to the ladies' room.

Then the unthinkable happened. I went to the bar to get yet another beer only to be told they stopped serving near the end of the third period. Whaaaaa? We have overtime. What the hell are we to do? I was almost on the verge of tears when I remembered a friend I had run into on the way into the stadium told me he watches the game at Hyde. I texted him, he met me outside the Hyde entrance and introduced me to the VIP host, who gave me her business card and let me in. I got a couple drinks and took them back to our suite and we were golden for overtime.

There were so many close calls for both teams but no one scored. We were going into double overtime, and now I'm taking drink orders from Hyde and playing waitress for the suite. In the second overtime Dustin Brown scored at around the nine-minute mark and you'd have thought that was the final game. We were high-fivin' and screaming our heads off. It felt good.

It was a good day.

The Kings beat the Rangers in game 3 at Madison Square Garden. As nervous as I was at the beginning of the series, I couldn't believe there was a chance of us sweeping this thing. How was that even possible? We LIVED for game 7. So when game 4 came around, don't tell nobody but I kinda wanted the team to lose so they could come back to LA and win it at home. Aaaand sure enough, we lost 2-1 in game 4.

Now it was time for game 5 and I had no expectations of getting in that arena. I had plans to do a late brunch out in Topanga Canyon and intended to watch the game at a Kings-friendly bar. I drove out to Topanga Canyon with my friend Rosa. We caravanned with two other cars to the Inn of the Seventh Ray for brunch. There were six adults and two kids. We were enjoying a lovely meal when at 2:46 p.m. I got a text from Heather:

Heather: Retta! NHL just came through with 2 for you in the box. Can you come?

Me: Yasssssss!!!!!

Heather: K—at valet

Me: Suh-weeeeeet!!!

Me: My heart is racing cuz we're "rushing" back from Malibu to change and catch the puck drop. God help us! I need to bang some shallow glass.

It was like I won the lottery. I asked Rosa if she wanted to go and she was like, hell yeah! We flew outta that restaurant so fast. And it is NOT a quick trip back to Hollywood from Malibu. I was so excited I could feel my heart beating in my chest. It took what felt like an eternity for us to get to our respective homes, and I got ready as fast as I could but I had to look as cute as possible #BecauseItsTheCup!

Needless to say, traffic was not our friend and we missed the puck drop. We entered the box to find it filled with hot guys: Nick Zano, Channing Tatum, Joshua Jackson, Joe Jonas, Oliver Hudson, and Wyatt Russell. Chloë Grace was back to represent as well. We also missed getting our front-row seat on the low glass of the box. Joe Jonas was in my seat. This made me nervous because, as I've said, I'm super-stitious and I was on the glass when we won game 2. Mr. Bett-man (The Commish) was back in the box and this time it was like we were old friends, at least for me. Rosa had taken to calling him Uncle Gary, which kept us both amused.

Anyway, the game started and we were not there long before mah boo, aka JDub aka Justin Williams, scored the first goal. This was the beginning of a lot of up and down for me. The Rangers scored the next two goals, and that's when I started to get antsy. I bounce my right leg when I'm nervous, and there was a whole lot of bouncing going on. Rosa kept saying, "I don't know, Retta. The Rangers are gooood." And KNOW that THAT made me craaaazy. I was like, you can't sit with me and say shit like that. I'm way too invested in this club to hear anything disparaging.

We tied it up about eight minutes into the third. There was a shot by the Rangers that hit the post and could've ruined my night but the puck bounced in our favor and I knew in my heart that this shit was going to overtime and I was STRESSED. Not just because we could lose but because I knew they had stopped serving alcohol!! So once again I was hitting up Hyde to retrieve my nerve juice, which for that night was vodka soda. Overtime was so stressful, but not as stressful as getting to the end of overtime and realizing we were once again going into a second overtime. Yes. A SECOND overtime. AGAIN.

I don't think I sat down once during the second overtime. My leg was shaking. I was wringing my hands. I was goin' THROUGH it. That second overtime felt like there were nothing but shots on the Kings' goal and God bless Quickie cuz he wasn't havin' it. But then it happened. With 5:17 left on the clock Martinez made the shot, and I thought I'd pass out from elation. Ho. Lee. Shit, we just won this goddamn game. Staples went batshit fucking crazy. I was screaming. Martinez was doing jazz hands on the ice. The team was rushing him. It. Was. Awesome.

So the original question was "Since when am I a hockey fan?" and the answer is the instant I was a part of that championship moment. It felt good and to think I might have missed out on it because my first instinct was *I ain't goin' all the way to Staples for hockey. I don't know shit about hockey.* Because I was able to keep an open mind and just go on an adventure I've had so many memorable opportunities. Those opportunities include:

- Presenting at two NHL Awards, where I met Luc Robitaille and Cam Neely

- Meeting the Keeper of the Cup

- Taking pictures with the Stanley Cup

- Live-tweeting EPIX's *Road to the NHL Stadium Series*

- Meeting Brent Burns, aka "Burnzie," while live-tweeting *Road to the NHL Stadium Series*

- Attending home games of the New York Rangers, Boston Bruins, Anaheim Ducks, and Dallas Stars

- Taking over NHL Snapchat for a night

- Appearing on *NHL Live*

And I got to present the Best Team Award to the Kings at Sports Spectacular's thirtieth annual awards show, where Luc told me and the audience gathered that they needed me back because they believe I'm good luck. I feel like he says this to a lot of people, but it still felt special.

As a Duke alum and Blue Devil fan who was in the stands at our last national-championship win away from Cameron Indoor Stadium, I can tell you there's nothing like being in your home stadium and having nearly all 18,000 fans in attendance lose their shit because their boys just did their damn thing. So, yes, I'm officially a hockey fan. Like a first-time gambler hitting the Vegas progressive jackpot with only a twenty-dollar bill, or a newbie winning a superfecta on their first trip to the track, it's been a perfect storm for a vuh-ry suh-rious problem. This unicorn is hooked! #GoKingsGo*

---

* A portion of this chapter first appeared as an article in my pals Jenni Konner and Lena Dunham's *Lenny* newsletter on May 11, 2016.

Chapter Fourteen

It's An UnfoRETTAble Life

L ike most people these days, the very first thing I do when I wake up is roll over and . . . CHECK SOCIAL MEDIA. Okay, maybe there's a quick toot* first, but my second natural reflex is to reach over and grab my phone from the nightstand. When I see my screen all fresh and fully charged, I smile and stretch my arms to the heavens like Sleeping Beauty awakening from her long slumber. I ask you: Does anything give you more of a sense of readiness than a phone at 100 percent? It's a feeling of being *capable* of handling business. But it is bittersweet, because we know it's fleeting. I think the scientist who figures out how to build a phone battery that lasts a week on one charge will be at the top of the list of Nobel candidates.

I start my morning-media routine thusly:

First, I check my @ mentions on Twitter because I like to see the comments. I'll reply to people who are funny because that's the reason I go on Twitter—I want to be amused.

---

* Don't judge. I am a human person.

Nothing makes me crazier than the people on Twitter who are like, "Follow me! It would make my life if you followed me!" Well, your life is really sad, and you need to get off the computer and make real-life friends. Or the ones who say, "Can you tell so-and-so I love her?" I am not so-and-so's message service. Or even worse, people who ask me where they should go for dinner or what they should do that night. I am not the cruise director of your life. Does it say *concierge* somewhere in my profile?

Second, I check my notifications on Facebook. I rarely ever look at my feed. Truth be told, I only keep my Facebook account out of respect for the platform . . . aaaand in the hopes that my former crushes find my page and see the cute pics of myself that I've posted. It's flawed but it's honest.

Third comes Snapchat. At first, I was against Snapchat. I didn't get it. But once my friend Brian Mahoney (li'l shout-out for @mahone_alone) taught me how to work it, I was hooked. It's where I document my coffee making and #No Pants life. It's like my own reality show produced by me! I also enjoy receiving Snaps from like-minded people. The #No Pants principle runs deep.

THE NO-PANTS LIFE

And, lastly, for a while it was important I check Instagram. Not just to see posts that I missed, but to check the number of followers I had. I could see that I was constantly getting followers but the number of followers on my account wouldn't change. There was no uptick. It started making me crazy.

Why hadn't my numbers gone up? And more important, when did I become a numbers whore? I had my publicist get in contact with the powers that be, the technical team, and they finally rectified the situation. I've since chilled a little. But here's an Instagram question for you: Who are these people that feel the need to comment "first"? What are you doing with your life other than refreshing your feed to see who else you can impress with your "first" comment? Half the time there are more than three people who have commented "first" and it gives me such satisfaction to delete their comments. I know it's stupid and serves zero purpose cuz no one is looking at your "first" comment going, "Wow, that CouchJockey929 has really got his shit together and is at the top of his game," but it provides the smallest amount of gratification for me.

It is a wicked pleasure. Picture me snickering conspiratorially, with no one . . . then dropping my phone on my face. Karma. THAT's what *that* is. I've gotten to that place where I have a bit of animosity toward social media* because I've dropped my phone on my face while lying in bed more times than I care to admit. It's like being salty with *Grand Theft Auto* cuz you developed carpal tunnel from playing it too much. Bitch, when you start getting injured by your phone you need to take a step back and think about what it is you are doing with your life. Put. The. Phone. Down.

Sheeeeee-it. Y'all know that ain't gon' happen, right?

---

* I might as well treat it like a real person since it's my most passionate relationship at the moment.

A few busted lips aren't gonna make me quit social media. I'll just put some ice on that bitch and keep awn typin'.

As we've seen, I have an addictive personality so I'm a prime target to become one of the 10 percent clinically addicted to their phones, aka a "smartphone abuser," which, by the way, is a little aggressive. I prefer the term "FOMOphobia."

I try to keep up with what's on social media. It's not like I'm checking what's trending every hour, but I do like to know what folks are posting about. When I hear news that I wanna know the deets on, the first place I check is Twitter. When there's a rumor that someone famous has died, I go to Twitter to see if reputable accounts like CNN or Newsweek are posting about it. I try my best to keep up with internet slang and shorthand. There's always some new shortcut or acronym on social media that prevents me from understanding a post: BAE, F2F, TBT, FBF, FOMO, FTW, HMU, ICYMI, IDK. It was all too much to keep up with. The first time I saw "seriously" written as "SRSLY," I thought, *Seriously?* Then, of course, I found myself using that shortcut because in the age of 140 characters, those few letters allow for a myriad of words. I'm trying to be accepting of this new "web-speak." It's taken me a minute. It took a while to come to terms with people calling me "MOM." I couldn't understand why so many people were leaving "MOM" comments on my posts. I started to get my feelings hurt. I thought they were calling me old. I finally had to google the internet meaning and found that it was an "expression of adulation," as in, you're so cool, I wish you were my mom. If it were small children saying it, it might not bother me. Although if it *were* small children saying it they'd likely be under parental supervision, in which case I'd feel supes uncomfortable, too. But it's "kids" old enough to have social media accounts . . . and apartments, so it just made me feel old.

I have my own style and techniques when it comes to social media-ing. For example, I like to capitalize the first letter of every word in a hashtag because I find it's easier to read. I don't wanna spend fifteen extra seconds trying to decipher #thisisjustcompleteandutternonsense.* I don't have that kind of time. I also tend to add spaces in my tweet. I don't know if it's more for ease of reading or to know I have a specific style. I DO know that *some* people don't appreciate it. Somebody once commented, "If you type your tweets like this, it takes up a bigger amount of space! You're a jerk!" It gave me pause, but I'm not exactly losing sleep.

It's scary how quickly people can turn on you, though. A few years ago I was watching *Mad Men* on my DVR when I tweeted this joke:

> Vegans make me uncomfortable same way non-drinkers do. When I order, I feel judged by & sorry 4 U @ the same time. #sorry #stillorderingit

The response from the Twittersphere was swift and mighty. I got into a major BEEF (rimshot!) with an army of vegans who piled on me after their dear leader @VeganNotFeelingRetta† retweeted it or just made it known how she felt about it.

---

* #ThisIsJustCompleteAndUtterNonsense

† I'm using a fake profile name to protect the innocent.

> **@VeganNotFeelingRetta:** @unfoRETTAble is a
> perfect example of why so many vegans are
> cranky. Sad, and sick.

> **@unfoRETTAble:** You know I'm a comedian,
> right?

> **@VeganNotFeelingRetta:** Don't feel sorry for
> vegans; feel sorry for the animals, the planet, your
> own temple for the damage done by said choices.

I made it known to her that I was a comedian and was tweeting a joke. Then her herbivore circle of friends @Retta MustBeTrippin and @Leaves4Life got in on the action:

> **Targeting vegans right now is the same as a
> comedian complaining about airplane food in the
> 90s—you're better than that** @unfoRETTAble

> @unfoRETTAble **your joke on vegans was so
> fuckin funny #welovejudgingmeateaters
> #fuckoutaherewithyourlameexcuseofbeinga
> comedian**

Okay, first off, the tweet got a hundred retweets so it was *kinda* funny, right?* Secondly, I get her point. She was fighting for what she stood for . . . but so was I, my online com-

---

* This was more than four years ago so I didn't have that many followers at the time.

edy, so I announced I was pausing *Mad Men* to deal with the hangry mob. My followers at the time were like, "Oh shit, Retta's pausing *Mad Men*, shit's about to go down! She's about to read some motherfuckers!" Okay, maybe that's how I *interpreted* their response, but whatever the case, I was amped.

> **How 'bout you get the fuck off my page.**
> **#BLOCKED**

Though the vegans came at me—making snide comments about my body *and* my comedy career—my loyal followers had my back with some decent one-liners:

> **They make me want to punch a hamburger in the face!**
> **You know they miss bacon!**
> **Fuck vegans!**

After an hour of insults back and forth, it started to get annoying, so it was time to take the figurative meat off the flame. I waved the white flag and offered a conciliatory message in a series of tweets:

> **As I am not getting a response, I am going to say this. I am not looking to take on Vegans. Some of my best friends are vegan. I made a joke and I'm not fucking apologizing for it. If you have an issue with that, go with God. You coming at me with my Twitter handle to make your meat hater point shall fall on deaf ears b/c as I mentioned ur only**

making the joke a reality. Now Ima gon' ahead
and finish #MadMen because that's what makes
me happy . . . and you can werrk your Kale salad
and do a fruit dance if that's what makes you happy
and we shall all enjoy our evening. @kevinrfree
has requested that I not engage but clearly it's
too late for that so I bid thee farewell. Again
#VegansDoYou Ima do me and, not gonna lie,
prolly some chicken strips. #PleaseRecycle
Back to our regularly scheduled program:
#MadMen

My clash with the vegans was mostly funny; it didn't go
to that dark, fucked-up place that's all too common online
these days. When *Ghostbusters* star Leslie Jones was targeted
with the most vile, racist tweets, just for starring in a movie,
I cried. For her, for me, for humanity. People can be fucking
disgusting, heartless monsters. I've been there. Recently I did
a digital ad, in the form of a GIF, for I Can't Believe It's Not
Butter, where they built a toaster that lasered my morning
refrain "Dark Maaagic"* on a piece of toast. Personally, I was
helluh impressed, but a couple of ladies (I hesitate to call them
that) didn't get it or particularly appreciate it and called me a
"monkey." A. Monkey. Why? Because a piece of toast had
some words on it? It's not that serious, Nancy, it's just a little
thing called "paying my mortgage." Fuckin' relax.

I've been called racist names plenty of times but it hasn't

---

* Dark Magic is a coffee distributed by Green Mountain. See chapter 2.

escalated to the level of hatred Leslie experienced. I usually look at the account to see if this is just the kind of thing they spew all the time (read: troll) and I either just block 'em or suggest they tell it to their twelve followers and then block 'em. There was a time, though, it very easily could have spiraled out of control. So here's the sitch. Anyone who knows me knows I'm big into live-tweeting. If I love a show, I'm gonna put my very important thoughts and reactions into 140 characters and unleash them into the Twitterverse. It all started when I was working on *Parks*. There's a lot of downtime when filming a show or movie. So I bought the DVDs for *Breaking Bad* to watch while in my trailer. And if you've watched the show, you know it's intense, thus it gave me a great deal of anxiety. So I started tweeting because it made me feel like I wasn't alone. My Twitter followers would often respond with, "It's okay! Don't worry! Stay with it, it'll be worth it!" It was comforting to know that others had been through the same stress and made it through to the other side.

Soon they started warning about things to come. "Wait till the next episode! You won't believe how Walter gets out of this one! Have you seen when . . ." At a certain point, I was like, *Stop tipping me off as to what's to come!* But people loooooove to be the first person to tell you something. I'm like, I haven't watched it yet, and now you just ruined it by telling me that whatchumacallit gets killed! Thanks, Mr. Overly Helpful. As much as I hated spoilers, I loved interacting with people while I was watching. Next thing I knew I was live-tweeting all my favorite shows, like *The Good*

Wife, *Game of Thrones*, *Vampire Diaries*, *Scandal*, and series re-visits like *Buffy the Vampire Slayer* and *Gilmore Girls*. I tweeted about so many shows, I kind of got a rep for being a good TV commentator (as I pop my collar). So I was to appear on *The Walking Dead*'s *Talking Dead*. Say that ten times fast.

Not everyone loved me or my opinions, like this dude from Fresno who complained about my tweets that AMC's *The Walking Dead* account had been retweeting. He replied all, just to make sure I'd see his comment:

Stop retweeting loud mouth black people!

Well, that's odd, I thought. How can you tell I'm loud? It's not like I'm typing in all caps. And who in the fuck are you, exactly? I retweeted what he said, blocked his ass, and went to sleep. When I woke up the next morning, I was bombarded with notifications. My followers had gone in deep on this guy, going back and forth, back and forth, back and forth all night. People were still using my handle in their tweets, so I could see what had gone down. My fans were ripping this guy a new one. They were also sending me screenshots of his account, which showed him using the word "nigger" like he was born to do it; a post of a black guy eating watermelon with his comment, "Figures"; and a picture he said was of him and his girlfriend in gorilla costumes, saying they went as Barack and Michelle Obama for Halloween. This guy was something special.

The best part about Fresno's account? The ignoramus posted about his job at at a large retail company, bragging about how he had just been promoted from an hourly gig to a straight salary. He was also one of those classy types who posted a bathroom selfie in a cheap suit to show off how *fancy* he was. One of my California followers offered to go to Fresno "to find this motherfucker." I magnanimously chose to ignore the offer. My favorite alert that morning was from Fresno's bosses. They had direct messaged me, saying, "We're aware of the situation and it is being taken care of." I unblocked Fresno to look at his account and all of the racist shit had been deleted. By the time I'd gotten through my @mentions, the whole account had been shut the F down. I suspect Fresno got fired. But I don't really know. What I do know is that it wasn't going to work out well for him. And listen, I'm not the type of person who wants people to lose their jobs. It's hard out here for a pimp, but I gotta say the only thing I could think was, *Bye Felicia*.

Twitter can be used not only for evil but also for good. Once I was on a flight to New York City and live-tweeted the movie *The Holiday*. So many people tried watching it on Netflix that Netflix got overloaded and it wouldn't load! Someone tweeted, "Oh my God, Retta, you crashed Netflix!" So maybe I wasn't solving the Israeli-Palestinian conflict, but I thought if this is the only way I make my mark, I'll take it. And, I'm not gonna lie, I loved the power. It was like an aphrodisiac. I assume this is what hackers experience or how trolls feel when they get strangers worked up over their nonsense.

I have taken advantage of the fact that at any given time I have an audience. Take the year NBC asked me to live-tweet the 66th Annual Emmy Awards. They'd given me a prime seat all the way up in the second row so I wouldn't miss anything going down with host Seth Meyers and I'd be within spitting range of the likes of Julia Louis-Dreyfus, Kevin Spacey, and Peter Dinklage. There'd been a seat-filler next to me at one point, but then this young guy came with a ticket during the second commercial break and the seat-filler got kicked out. So this guy sat next to me and I heard him on the phone like, "Where are you? I'm at our seats." Whatever the situation was, I think his date was in a different place in the theater. He got off the phone and turned to me.

"I think you're in my girlfriend's seat," he said.

"Uh, I don't think so." And P.S., guess who was here first, homie?

"Can I see your ticket?"

The fuq?

"No, you cannot see my ticket."

He called the usher over. "I was supposed to be sitting with my girlfriend and I think this is her seat," pointing to *my* seat.

I pulled out my ticket and I held it to my left to show the usher cuz the annoying guy was on my right. I showed it to her and she was like, "You're in the right seat. I wouldn't get up." And I was like, "I'm *not*!"

I didn't get up and the usher left. About five minutes later, I heard his gums flapping again.

"Can I see your ticket?"

"Dude, this is MY seat. My ticket is for THIS seat."

To shut him up, I finally showed him my fucking ticket. It said "Orchestra." His said "Mezzanine."

"I think you're in the wrong seat," he said, "because it says 'Orchestra.' "

"Excuse me, have you been to the theater before? Do you know where the orchestra is? The orchestra's on the floor. Your seat is back there."

Now he realized he was in the wrong seat. He realized he was so lucky to get by security and be up so close, and he quickly decided there was no way he's givin' up this cush locale, girlfriend be damned. He was taking pictures of everything and during commercial breaks tryna talk to me.

"So what do you do?"

Are you fucking kidding me right now? "I'm an actor."

"Anything I've seen?"

"I don't know what you watch, homie. I'm on *Parks and Recreation*."

"Oh yeah, I was supposed to be an extra on that once. I never watched it, I hear it's supposed to be good."

At the next commercial break, he cornered me.

"Do you think you could get me work as an extra on your show? Once I was an extra and they bumped me up and I got a line."

You just fucking showed up here late, claimed I was in your girlfriend's seat, realized *you're* in the wrong seat, won't leave, and now you're asking me for extra work?

"Let's take a picture," he said. He raised his phone for a selfie and I was stone-faced. "What's your Instagram?"

"Dude, I'm not giving you my Instagram."

"We should be friends."

"I don't know you."

"You know me now, we're sitting with each other at the Emmys!"

"Yeah, no, we're good."

He was so fucking annoying I got up to go to the bathroom and I told the ushers, "He's in the wrong seat, he's annoying me and he needs to fucking GO." By the time I came back out of the bathroom, security was walking him out. Not sure where to. Probably to his *actual* seat.

Here's the kicker, I was live-tweeting the entire time, of course. One of those sites like Popsugar or Jezebel had been following the encounter and by the time the awards were over had posted the whole story. Other sites started reporting on it. The next day, somebody must have been like, "Dude, they're talking about you," because he had posted our selfie. He then took to Twitter and started FAT-SHAMING me. Tweeting shit like "You took up two seats"—that kind of thing. "I only posted your picture so everybody could see how fucking fat and gross you are." Really? Is that why you asked me to be your friend on Instagram? Anyway. I retweeted all of his nasty tweets because, clearly, he wanted to be heard.

The story got picked up by several major media sites like *Huffington Post*, *E! Online*, and BuzzFeed, all of which went after him like the real-life troll he was. The *Los Angeles Times* fucked up that day, though, mixing me up with Danielle Brooks from *Orange Is the New Black*, because, you know, we all look alike. I wasn't about to let that shit go, so I tweeted the paper, "Ooohhhh @LATimes . . ." with a screen grab of their gaffe. They sent both me and Danielle flowers apologizing, so I posted a picture of the flowers with the message, "I accept your apology @NewYorkTimes."

Now that would be a good ending to this story but it ain't over yet. The guy found me on Instagram (it's not that hard) and sent me a message. No, not "first," though he seems like that type. He wrote, "Can I have your address I want to send you an apology, too."

Here's my reply: "Dude, if you don't fucking stop stalking me I'm going to report you to the police. Get the fuck off my feed." And I blocked him. Again, Bye Felicia. I was so pissed. It was entitlement at its best.

I've had some amusing adventures online as well. I had this whole thing with Joe Manganiello, which unfortunately was way less sexy than it sounds. I used to live-tweet *True Blood* and I loved Alcide—what's not to love? He was a broody, sensitive werewolf, and his body was ridiculous. So I would tweet stuff about it and one time he responded, "You might be my favorite person on Twitter."

I responded, "Hahaha. That's awesome. Glad you like. P.S. this totes makes u my boyfriend & I intend to tell errybody I'm boning Alcide."

We laughed. Or I guess we just Lol'd.

Then my friend Yvette Nicole Brown ran into him at Comic Con, took a picture, and tweeted it to me with the message, "Hey @unfoRETTAble! Found your boyfriend, @joemanganiello ;) #JealousMUCH?"

I replied, "Nah, not really b/c Joey & I know what we have. And yeah 'Joey' 'cause that's where WE'RE at. Nicknames."

We continued with this foolishness which amused us BOTH until Octavia Spencer got in on the fun. She'd done a movie with him in the past and wanted to know why he was two-timing her. It escalated to where the media was writing articles about us "fighting" over Joe. Our back-and-forth had gotten to a point that when I cohosted the talk show *Anderson Live with Anderson Cooper*, the producers had made this giant pillow with a picture of Joe that I could hug to fall asleep. And Joe was playing along, at one point writing, "Ladies, ladies, there's enough of me to go around!"

All harmless fun. But the moment I knew that people were really invested in this foolishness was when he started dating *Modern Family* star Sophia Vergara and *US Weekly* contacted me for comment. I was like, "Y'all know this was a joke, right??" They did but still wanted comment. I obliged.

"It is with a heavy heart that I learn of Joe Manganiello aka my wolfy Twitter boo is seeing one Ms. Sofia Vergara. As with any (pretend) conscious uncoupling there is still much love and my Mellow Nello (that was what I called my boo in my head) will always hold a special place in my Twitter heart."

I've had some learning experiences on social media as well. Once while live-tweeting *Orange Is the New Black*, I called transgender actress Laverne Cox "he/she." I know, I KNOW. I had NO IDEA she was a transgender actress. It was the episode where we learn her character's backstory. I thought she was playing her pre-op self, which, after some research, I found was her actual brother. Someone tweeted, "Whoa, people are gonna come after you." And boy did they come after me. Even though I was unaware of the *actual* circumstances, I was actually ignorant as to the struggle/feelings of transgender individuals. Twitter made this a teaching moment for me and I did indeed learn.

I also had a tiff with feminists, of which I consider myself one. I was coming home from work late one night and I was taking side streets to avoid Sunset Boulevard traffic. I was on a really dark street that basically had no lights. There was a girl jogging and I tweeted out something along the lines of, "What the fuck are you doing jogging on this street? It's helluh dark out here. I don't even want to drive on this street."* These feminists came at me saying she should be able to run wherever she wants. I get your point, feminists. We need to change rape culture rather than limit the freedoms of women. I think I should be able to run in the dark naked if I want to, but right now where we are in our society, I don't think it's a *wise* choice. If I had a daughter, I wouldn't tell her to run where and when she wanted because it was her right. Not because I don't think it is her right, but because it is more important to me that she stay safe.

It's like when the police tell black folks to "put your hands up" when you know you didn't do anything. I mean, black parents aren't telling their children, "You have equal rights so if you feel like you're being arrested for some shit you didn't do, stand up for yourself." You're right, you shouldn't be arrested for some shit just for being black but, by the way, I'm not trying to get shot, either. We're not at that place yet. It's not a safe world. For as much as we love our country and the freedoms that come with being here, we all know it's not true for everybody.

My thing is if I feel like you're right, I'm gonna say it. I'm not too smart to learn a lesson. I'm gonna be like, you're right and my excuse is I didn't know. I'd like to think that I'm pretty accepting and pretty liberal, but if someone calls me out on

---

* I posted it when I got home. Don't tweet and drive, kids.

my shit I'm gonna take the time to hear and respond accordingly. You know what I mean?

I never talk politics because that is too often a lose-lose situation. I did a benefit show for Hillary Clinton and some Bernie zealots came for me. They were like, "I'm so disappointed in you. I thought you were better than that." I was like, hold the fuck up. I am not your child and you don't *know* me. I hold no role in your life other than I'm an entertainer that you perhaps enjoyed on a television show at one point. I hold no other position in your life. For you to have feelings of disappointment in me denotes a level of intimacy we do not and have never had. And P.S., we have differing political leanings. Disappointed in me? I'm not hiding children in my basement.

Another time I posted a picture of me wearing a T-shirt that Lena Dunham designed for Planned Parenthood. Good Lord, the comments. I was like, you guys, I don't care how you feel about me, I think women have rights and I'm backing Planned Parenthood. All you have to do to show you disagree is hit unfollow, that's it. "Unfollow" is your friend just as "block" is *my* muhfuhkuh. I'm not gonna get in an argument with you on MY timeline because you learned something in church that I disagree with. I just posted this pic cuz my hair and makeup were on point.

Bottom line is I really just want to have fun on my social media. I like to tell my little jokes and keep up with what my friends are up to. If I can watch Dr. Pimple Popper get at some sebaceous cysts and Paris Hilton go on and on about how much she loves Ibiza, I'm happy. I'll post my coffee making, throw in a few jokes, and call it a day. That's all I want. I'm not interested in going back and forth with you about whether or not Trump speaks the truth.

Can't we all just get along? And if not, can we at least be civil human beings?

BTW, Trump is a demagogue only interested in self-aggrandizement.*

---

* There's no comment section in this book, haters! *Nanh nanh nuhnanh nanh!* Also, this book was written before he won and before I took more of a political stand on social media.

Chapter Fifteen

Stretch Marks fo Life!

I hate my arms.

I didn't always hate my arms. I mean, they won me medals in high school for the shot put, give outstanding hugs, and proficiently carry my prized handbags. But the heavier I got over the years, the bigger my arms got, until finally, about fifteen years ago, at size 28, I had to come to an unfortunate decision: I would no longer wear anything sleeveless, until further notice or hell froze over.

My fellow fashionistas out there know how severely that can limit a gal's wardrobe. So many staples come sans sleeves—from bathing suits to tank tops to sundresses, not to mention the most gorgeous of gowns. Sometimes I had no choice but to go sleeveless. Like when you're a bridesmaid (see chapter 6). It is a thankless job and your costume choices should be your own. Or on a red carpet, and when that happened, I'd make do as best I could. I'd wear a shawl, a scarf, or a little sweater to cover up my ample appendages.

That ploy seemed to work, maybe not like a charm but it was FINE. I got by for a time. Until one spring day, I, along with my female *Parks* costars, was named to *People* magazine's "50 Most Beautiful" list. A most flattering honor, of course;

I'd be joining an elite club that includes the likes of Julia Roberts and Kerry Washington and George Clooney. But I wasn't quite so flattered when I showed up to the photoshoot and the stylist wanted to put Amy, Rashida, Aubrey, and me in pale sleeveless gowns. Here I was, about to be on the most famous listicle of attractiveness, and my arms, not my favorite attribute but definitely my *least* favorite attribute,* would be visible to *People*'s 40-plus million readers. You'd never know it by looking at the pic that made it in the magazine, showing us goofing around a croquet set in a lush green garden, but I was so self-conscious about my exposed arms I dreaded the day the issue would come out.

That photoshoot did a number on my self-esteem but wasn't the wake-up call that got me moving, literally. Not surprisingly, it took getting dumped by a guy to give me the motivation I needed. That's not completely true. It was my bestie Rosa who got me started, and it was this not-so-conscious uncoupling that kept me steadfast in my endeavor.

About a year after the sleeveless *People* incident, I got totally ghosted. This dude and I were planning a vacation together but suddenly out of nowhere he was posting pics of a girl I'd never met or heard about on Facebook. I didn't know if something was for sure going on but it didn't feel kosher. I decided I wouldn't call him and I'd wait until he called me. He didn't. I never heard from him again.

Needless to say, a bitch was salty. Salty, sad, and, not gonna lie, a little humiliated. I felt like shit. I wanted to call him and be like, What. The. Fuck. Dude? Really? But I didn't. I at least

---

* *P & R* fans get it.

committed to putting him/us in my past. That and to sticking to my workouts and food management with Rosa. I was gonna lose weight. Not for that dumb ass, but for myself (though, who are we kidding, looking good is the best revenge). I was committing to my regimen. Big-time. Working out. Hard. I'd already been doing some cardio in the pool at the Y but it wasn't enough. Rosa had been house-sitting for Josh Gad, star of Broadway's *The Book of Mormon* but probably better known to the parents out there as the voice of Olaf in *Frozen*. He had a nice pool and turns out she wanted to, as we put it, get in Bey shape. We created our own water workout based on things we'd done before and exercises we found online.

I am grateful for so many of my friends. Rosa is one of them. We met through mutual friends some years ago at a bar and have been laughing ever since. We connect on a different level. We have similar backgrounds in that we are both Jersey girls (although we met in LA) who grew up with immigrant parents. We understand having an outside American life and going home to an "old-country" life. We have similar senses of humor and similar vulnerabilities. Rosa is very much like my mother in that she loves to feed people and loves opening her home to people. I didn't appreciate that quality as a kid but I see the goodness in it. Rosa has taught me generosity. She's also taught me boundaries cuz you can be *too* generous. She makes me laugh and she makes me blush because she can be as filthy as an ex-marine. She's as perfect a ride-or-die as you're gonna find.

On July 31, 2014, Rosa and I hopped on over to Sport Chalet and cleaned out the joint. We got all sorts of aquatic equipment, like floatie belts and pool weights and webbed resistance gloves and cute little bathing caps to match our bathing suits, and, most important, Fitbits to make sure we were walking 15,000 steps per day. We promised ourselves if we met our weight-loss goals, we'd treat ourselves to Tory Burch's cute new gold metal bracelets meant to hold the Fitbit. With all our aqua gear we went in and we went in *hard*. We worked out for two hours every day. Sometimes longer. And we did it seven days a week for two months. In that water, treading for six minutes at a time, alternating with two minutes of abs, arms, legs, and running. I'd been following comedian Kevin Hart on Instagram. He's helluh fit and posts a gang of vids of him working out and often uses the hashtag #HustleHart. As a nod to his commitment to staying fit, whenever we got to the point in our workout where we had to run our hardest we'd say, "Hustle Hart!" That meant go hard, bitch.

We never wavered in our commitment. I attribute this to three things:

1. When Rosa puts her mind to something she sticks to it, and I'm codependent so I liked knowing I had company every day.

2. At the end of the workout, we'd sit in the hot tub and commiserate about the dudes who fucked us over. Free therapy. I came to realize Ghosty McVanished wasn't my future. He'd never been. Never could be.

3. Once you start seeing results, you look forward to doing the work.

To make sure we were staying within our daily calorie allotment, we downloaded the app MyFitnessPal and followed it as if our lives depended on it. I didn't cut out any specific foods. I just tried to eat like I had some damn sense. I'd set an alarm to make sure I ate every few hours and made especially sure that I didn't go over my allotted calories per day based on my step count. That number fluctuated daily, but I can tell you that at a certain point I was up to 100,000 steps per week and was allowed 2,400 calories per day, so I certainly wasn't going hungry. I still didn't cook, so I just chose restaurants where I could feasibly count calories or look up the calorie count online—places like Tender Greens or Fresh Corn Grill so I knew exactly what to add into MyFitnessPal. This system allowed us to go to places like The Cheesecake Factory and get the light pasta and split a butter cake* because we knew exactly what the calories were. As long as we were under the calorie count, it was pretty much anything goes.

Maybe that sounds crazy. After all, it's food that got me in this predicament. In high school, I was on the track team and a cheerleader but as soon as I left for college, I packed on the pounds. First, it was the typical freshman fifteen . . . *plus*. Then, during my junior year, I injured my knee running track and stopped exercising for a really long time. And then when I broke my ankle in that deck collapse in LA it all went to shit. Add onto that all the booze and binge-eating I've done— short ribs, lasagna, fast food—and that adds up fast and permanently. I got to the point of no return, size 28, where

---

* If you've never had the butter cake at Cheesecake Factory, do yourself a favor. And if you've never had it at Mastro's, Get. It. You will love me, then curse me.

literally nothing fit me and getting all that weight off my body was going to take a monumental effort.

But that never meant starving myself. I *did* try the Atkins diet for about five minutes before I decided I'd rather die a fiery death at sea than give up bread. And I did Herbalife for a hot second until I realized that the "tea" that was keeping me so motivated was packed with caffeine and I legit thought I was gonna have a heart attack. I never hit the cayenne pepper–syrup water stage or the mashed-up baby-food plan. That's not real life. I don't care if Beyoncé *did* lose twenty pounds on it. You can't keep that shit up forever. Slow and steady wins the race.

Having said that, it ain't easy to get healthy and it's too easy to give up. Not even a week into our workout, feeling like Wonder Woman and Xena, Warrior Princess, we went to Bey and J's *On The Run* concert at the Rose Bowl. Well, the Uber driver had to drop us off about a mile away, and by the time I got up to the stadium, I was sweating and heaving as though I'd just raced Katie Ledecky in the 1,500-meter freestyle and *won*. My legs were on fie-errr and my makeup had slid off my face. I went into the bathroom to clean up, but was so wiped out, I noticed in the mirror on the way out I had little pieces of toilet paper stuck all over my face from trying to sop up the copious sweat. I looked fucking crazy, sweaty and gross. Still had a long way to go.

About a month in, after weighing myself four times a day even though everyone and their mother says don't, I was feeling good about what I had accomplished so far. And that's when I went to the Emmys, thinking I was cute, and encountered that asshole who tried to fat-shame me on social media, saying I filled up two seats. Little did he know I was on a path and his insults were only fuel to my fat-burning fire. I had started seeing results and was full-steam ahead. I was doing the damn thing.

Two months after Rosa and I started, are you ready? I lost FIFTY FUCKING POUNDS. Went from a size 28 to an 18. I was feeling myself more than Kanye feels Kanye. I online-shopped like it was end of days and filling one's virtual cart was the only way to keep Armageddon at bay. I got rid of a lot of stuff, too. Not everything, just the size 28s. I knew there was a chance I'd gain some weight back but I also knew in my heart I'd never go back to that place again.

Sure enough, when I started back at *Parks and Rec* for Season 7 and I couldn't fit two hours of exercise into my day, I went back up to a size 22 (some size 20 jeans) and that's where I remain today. I'm a super-organized person, but that's different from being disciplined. If I was disciplined, I'd be the size I want to be and I'm not. I catch myself eating crap late at night. I'm notorious for going an entire day without eating and then filling up on some nonsense just before hopping into bed. I still love my short ribs and starchy potatoes and corn. I still find tofu creepy. I'm trying to eat more vegetables and replace red meat with fish here and there. White fish, that is. Salmon can kiss my ass. And I'm lactose intolerant but if you told me I couldn't have cheese ever again, I would slap you in your face.

Hey, it's hard to lose weight when you like delicious food. Shit, it's hard to lose weight when you like shitty food.

Working out is great—it's the bonus—but, bottom line, it's the food. If I can wrap my mind around committing to counting calories for the rest of my life, maybe I'll get there. The biggest lesson I've learned from this whole ordeal is that what I really want is not the skinniest body, it's to live a life where I can just be a normal human being. There are plenty of people in the world who are fit who don't punch in the food they eat on their phones every ten minutes.

Will I ever be one of those people? Doubtful. I don't care anymore. Even though I've gained much of the weight back, I'm not as upset about it as I would have been before. I wanna look cute but I've gotten to a point where I've found decent clothes for a fat girl so I don't ever feel like I don't look cute. This is who I am.

I intend to lose more weight. I gotta get back to that if only for the health and well-being of my raggedy-ass knees, but right now I'm going to enjoy my life. You have to be happy in your regular life or you're not going to survive the journey toward a goal. It's the same with weight loss, you still have to be content. If you're miserable the whole time, it's gonna be too hard. You'll get to that point where you say "fuck it" and go ham on the entire contents of your fridge.

I had to come to a place in my mind where I'm okay with where I'm at. Once you do that, the good stuff happens. You present as more confident to the world. My girlfriends tell me that Mr. McPhantom always likes the pics they post with me in it. All I can say is WHATEVUH. On to the next. You do you, boo. I'ma do me.

I get called fat on Twitter all the time. It used to bother

me but now I'm like, "That's all you got? Trust me when I say you're not the first, you won't be the last. I'm gonna need you to be a little more creative, papi."* I wish when I was younger I'd had an awareness of how *un*clever and lazy it is to call somebody fat. It might've saved me so much heartache.

And, finally, I've made peace with my body. When I was drying my hair one day recently I was like, holy shit! I can see my collarbone for the first time in my life! I can cross my legs like a motherfucking LADY. And, yes, my ARMS. Are they Michelle Obama-worthy wings of glory? Yeah, no. They are fleshy and they are striped with the stretch marks of this lived life. But the ban has been lifted and I'm rocking the sleeveless again by CHOICE. I went to the U.S. Open with my arms out. I went to the Film Independent Spirit Awards with my guns blazing. And that made me feel cool

1. because it was hot as balls at both the Open and the Spirit Awards but . . .

2. . . . more important, because I felt good about it.

I can't say every day when I wake up I'm happy with my body, but I can say that every day when I wake up I'm happy *for* my body. We've been through a lot of shit together and I plan on going through a lot more. So if you see me out sporting a sleeveless look, know I broke out the big guns cuz I could.

---

* It's always a dude.

FOOD FOR THOUGHT*

1. I don't love arugula.

2. Finding pickles on a burger or sandwich that I specifically ordered WITHOUT pickles triggers a near psychotic break.

3. I'm partial to a pork dumpling.

4. I hate myself. But I still love bread.

5. Bread gives me a socially acceptable reason to eat *butter*. And for that I am grateful.

6. We get it, asparagus. No need to remind us that we just ate you. Stop taking over my urine scent.

7. Who is doing the PR for kale? And how can I get down with this company? Because kale used to be some bullshit underneath the salsa bins at Baja Fresh. Now it's the headliner on every menu. And Brussels sprouts are right behind them. They must have the same PR team.

8. Atlanta + Pimento Cheese. Someone please explain.

9. Am I alone in feeling that cookies, if broken, somehow have less calories?

10. There should be more mini quiche at parties.

11. I'd cut a bitch for some capellini bolognese.

12. Was anyone brave enough to order the Fritos Chicken Enchilada Melt at Subway? I couldn't bring myself to even say the words out loud.

---

* Second and last obligatory list that apparently is a big hit with these types of essay books. These are past tweets about food.

13. Ummm, why have y'all been tryna keep pretzel M&M's a secret? #Haters.

14. Was once so anxious over an episode of *The Good Wife* that I ate an expired bag of popcorn.

15. Do white people eat pork rinds?

16. I'm not mad at bacon.

17. I'm embarrassed by how far I'll drive for some fried chicken.

18. Sorghum "syrup" can kiss my ass. You ain't syrup.

19. I don't care how many times you say it's "edible." If you eat the rind of Brie I'm gonna look at you funny.

20. Marie Antoinette would've been executed a lot faster if she'd said, "Let them eat carrot cake."

21. I decided to make the healthier choice to exercise and eat better, but I gotta be honest, at this point I want Krispy Kreme more than I want children.

22. Fact: I'm at an age where what I have to do tomorrow dictates what I eat today. Dairy WILL delay a production schedule.

23. It is cruel that God gave me an unhealthy obsession w/ cheese AND made me lactose intolerant.

24. I always eat like I mean it. Just ask that Cornish game hen. He fuckin' knew I meant it.

Chapter Sixteen

That Year I Went Lin-Sane

Now that we're practically BFFs, you know that when I like something, I throw myself into it 1,000 percent (as long as I can do it from my couch). I've got a predilection for addiction, in the form of handbags, coffee, and tweeting. A fondness for Fassbender, a hunger for hockey, and TV binges. But that's small potatoes compared to the obsession that took over my life this past year.

I blame Josh Gad. Remember, Rosa and I had been exercising in his pool while he and his family were in Europe? One day, after they returned home from their vacay, Josh came out to the backyard to talk to us while we worked out. He was excited to tell us about their trip and about a musical he had just seen at The Public Theater in New York. His friend and Carnegie Mellon classmate Leslie Odom Jr. was one of the leads. He went on and on about how great the show was and how it wasn't like anything he'd seen before and the guy who wrote it was a genius, blah, blah blah. I probably would've been more engaged if my glutes hadn't been on fire from all the scissor kicks I was doing.

"I'm telling you," he insisted, "it's gonna change Broadway."

I took this opportunity to take a break and started listening. I mean, Josh *had* been nominated for a Tony so he prolly knew WTF he was talking about. He was so insistent that I *had* to look into it. I'm not exactly a big Broadway-head but I had recently started hittin' up shows whenever I traveled to New York City for work. Rosa had been a theater major in college so she generally steered me toward what was supposed to be hot on the Great White Way. So I texted my publicist, Tej, and asked her to look into tickets for my next work trip to Manhattan, not knowing at this early stage, even though it was still off-Broadway, it was easier to get Adele to perform at my godson's bris.

She said sure and I didn't think another thing about it. When the alert for my trip out to NYC popped up on my phone a week before travel, I texted Tej to see if she had secured tix. She had not. She said it was impossible. She'd been trying but was getting nowhere. I was like, "Word?" What is up with this show?

I googled it. *Hamilton*, created by and starring Lin-Manuel Miranda, was set to make its Broadway debut at the Richard Rogers Theatre in Times Square on August 6, 2015. Lin had already won a gang of awards for his groundbreaking 2008 Best Musical *In the Heights* and had been nominated for a Pulitzer. Apparently, he wasn't done blowing people's minds and his next undertaking was a brilliant musical extravaganza about the life of Alexander Hamilton and his fellow founding homies, all played by actors of color. It was a revolutionary collision of hip-hop and history. And, true to Josh Gad's word, the show was being regaled as the next big thing to head to Broadway. I wanted to go there.

If I had been nonchalant about getting in to see this show before, I was a little more than curious now. Since it was moving to Broadway, I told Tej not to sweat it and I would just get tickets once it opened there. The theater would be bigger and the tickets abundant.*

My New York trip came and went and I saw *The Audience* with Helen Mirren. She was fantastic. The show was well done. I thoroughly enjoyed it, but I still wanted to see this *Hamilton*. I contacted my publicist again and told her to just get me tickets, any tickets, and I would get a flight to New York. It didn't have to coincide with work obligations. She said she'd never experienced anything like this, but she wasn't going to stop until she got me those tickets. I had consigned myself to the reality that I might never see this play when out of the blue, the *Hamilton* PR assistant got back to Tej. He had seen my name in Tej's email request, was a big fan of *Parks*, and could rustle up four tickets for the final preview before the show opened if I wanted them. First of all, let's talk about how:

1. I got the tickets to the show because I had been on *Parks and Rec* (another reason I'm grateful to Mike Schur) and . . .

2. he was giving me FOUR tickets! FOUR!

I was like, fuck yeah, I'll take 'em! I knew Rosa was in, I just needed to find two more people who wanted to go, which

---

* Those of you who know about *Hamilton* KNOW how foolish this thought was.

was surprisingly difficult. The show had buzz but it was all inside-baseball kinda chatter in the theater community. I texted a guy I had a crush on and invited him.

> Do you want to go see Hamilton? It'd be nice to
> see you.

Mind you, I'd been trying to hook up with this guy in New York ever since I'd met him six months before but he'd always flaked on me. He turned me down. He was a musician and he didn't want to pay for show tickets. Mind you, these were house tickets, $176 each, a bargain since normal tickets were at minimum a grand for the seats I had—seventh row on the motherfucking aisle. I would have paid for him but I didn't want him to get weird about it. Guys can get weird about money shit and since I was still hoping to get back in his pants at some point, I just said no worries and kept it movin'. I invited a friend from college who's a New York actor but he was doing a show down in DC. I invited my lit agent who got me the deal to write this book you are reading and she *wanted* to go but didn't think she should leave work, as it was a matinee performance. We couldn't give these tickets away. We ended up taking Rosa's brother Rico and her cousin Francesca. I was rolling deep with the Graziano clan.

On the big day, from the moment I got out of the hotel shower until we were in our seats, I'd been snapping and Instagramming. We were v. excited and I was at my social media finest.

The energy in the room was off the charts. Just before the lights went up for the opening,* I started to panic. What if this shit didn't live up to the hype? Cuz I've had that experience before with other overly hyped shows. I'd once sat through a performance of a Tony Award–winning musical thinking, "This is it? *This* is what everyone's been losing their shit over?" I flew cross-country and got a hotel room to see THIS show and all I knew about it was that Josh had said it was gonna change Broadway. Plus, I wasn't seeing Lin in the leading role of Alexander Hamilton. His understudy, Javier Muñoz, was performing that afternoon.

The lights went up, and Leslie, who played Aaron Burr, entered the stage with a question: "How does a bastard, orphan, son of a whore and a Scotsman, dropped in the middle of a forgotten spot in the Caribbean by providence impoverished in squalor, grow up to be a hero and a scholar?"

By the end of the opening number I was IN and by the time Jonathan Groff finished his first number as King George, I was fucking OBSESSED. He was so charming yet despicable and funny that every subsequent time he stepped onstage I started to giggle. By the middle of the second half, we were broken. Rosa and I. Bawling. *Hamilton* was heartbreaking. Hilarious. Mind-blowing. Life-giving. Beautiful beyond words. The story, dancing, the rapid-fire lyrics—Daveed Diggs, who played Marquis de Lafayette and Thomas Jefferson, was killin' Lin's rhymes—filled my heart with joy, then smashed it to pieces.

---

* There's no curtain at *Hamilton*. You can see the stage the entire time.

After the show, the kid who got me the tickets, the cherub sent from on high, came up and introduced himself and took us onstage to meet the cast. That afternoon we met Daveed, Leslie, Okieriete "Oak" Onaodowan, and George Washington himself, Chris Jackson. They were all lovely and kind, and put up with my gushing as if it were the first time they'd heard the accolades. We hung around onstage for a bit, chatting and taking pictures with these gentlemen, when I saw Lin. All I could think was THIS is the guy. The mind behind what had made my heart soar for the past two hours and thirty minutes. He and some of the cast were sitting on the stage talking to a group of high school students about art and theater. I so wanted to meet him but I didn't want to bother him and we had a dinner reservation. So I left. Well, my body left. My heart, my mind, and my soul stayed in that theater for the next twenty-four hours.

Rosa and I couldn't stop talking about what we'd just seen. There was no cast album yet so we looked up clips online and recorded snippets for our Flipagram posts. Even Rico couldn't stop raving about it. "Dude, it fucking changed our lives!" he said in that masculine, Italian-guy-from-Jersey way.

My life was never the same, either. The next day I tweeted my "review" of the show.

> **My review of @HamiltonMusical:**
> It was so so so so good. It made me so happy. I
> laughed I smiled I bawled. It was Out. Of. Control.
> I wanna have Lin's babies.

I want Javier by my side as a life partner.
I wanna collab w/Leslie and star with him in
everything.
I wanna have dirty unabashed sex with Daveed.
I wanna hang with Oak at all things cool.
I wanna be best friends with Jonathan Groff and
have him serve as my Maid of Honor.
I wanna live on that stage and have each
and every one of them in my life forever and
always.
If someone says do you want to go see Hamilton
slap them in the face for asking such an
asinine question because it is an insult to your
sense of art culture and general
#KnowingGoodShit-ness.
So. Fucking. Good.
If I don't see it 4 more times it's because I've died
a sudden tragic death and in my last breath I
whispered Go. See. Hamilton.

I was already a woman possessed but my brainwashing was complete when I received my first tweet back from Leslie. He wrote:

@unfoRETTAble We. Loved. Having. You. Thank
you for the tweets. As funny as you are, people
take you hella seriously. These will matter. x

Then—drum roll please—Lin responded.

@Lin_Manuel **But how can I even thank** @
unfoRETTAble **for her kindness? *names first born
Lil' Sebastian*** YOU'RE 500 CANDLES IN THE WIND . . .
#thankyou

@unfoRETTAble: @Lin_Manuel **I loved it & cannot
wait to come see U as A. Ham! And just an FYI
I'm telling everyone ur my BFF. (U still my BBF** @
Rosagrazz.**)**

Sebastian *is* his son's name and Li'l Sebastian is Pawnee's
famous mini-horse on *Parks*! Lin watched *Parks*, which I
didn't know, and then I realized he'd already been following
me on Twitter!

@Lin_Manuel: @unfoRETTAble @Rosagrazz
Retta. **I was tweeting Buffy while** YOU **were
tweeting Buffy & yours were so good** I STOPPED
to read yours. WE ARE BFFS.

That's when I became obsessed with Lin because OMG
he is the greatest pop-culture nerd/regular old nerd EVER. We
ended up becoming pseudo-Twitter friends.*

I hearted my new friendship and all I could think about
was getting back to New York to see *Hamilton* with Lin IN
IT. That was my fucking goal. Every time I had to go back

---

* Lin might have had a different understanding of our "friendship," but
as far as I was concerned it was fate that brought us together and what
God has joined, let no man put asunder; we were besties!

for work, I'd ask my publicist, "Can you try to get me tickets again?" At this point, I was also asking the kid who had hooked me up the first time. I was like a junkie lookin' for a fix. I'm pretty sure he regretted giving me his email address. He was like, "Listen. Ima do what I can. Trust me when I say, it ain't easy. Okay?"

Okay.

It was his way of saying *get to the back of the line, Thirsty.*

I *got* it, but I was not to be thwarted. While I waited, I could satiate myself with the cast album, which I'd preordered and which automatically downloaded upon release. I remember being in the pool again, this time at my place and by myself when I saw it pop up in my iMusic. While I was working out, I listened to it on my Bluetooth. It was as though the entire show was playing out in my head and I was reliving the whole thing again. "Satisfied." "Helpless." "The Room Where It Happens." "Guns and Ships."

Rosa texted me.

> **Rosa:** Just walking the dog (☺☹) listening to the soundtrack. Every line is quotable.
>
> **Me:** oh my god. boo hooing in the pool right now!!!
>
> **Rosa:** Lol. We r so same person. I mean every line (crying emoji)
>
> **Retta:** I literally have a lump in my throat

Hearing Lin sing, all of that emotion. Reliving Leslie's incomparable buttery voice. And the women. THE WOMEN. It was almost as though I was hearing *them* for the first time.

How had I not gotten how deep these women went? Renée Elise Goldsberry's breath control alone was enough to take *my* breath away. I knew I had to get back. My obsession to see it again relaunched. The next time I was in the city, to tape *Late Night with Seth Meyers*, my publicist was like, "We should just go by the theater." That's how a lot of people get tickets because people drop out at the last minute. So we stopped by and nada. Zilch. I tweeted my utter devastation and disappointment. Next thing I know, Oak, aka Hercules Mulligan, tweeted me back.

I got you boo. DM me.

I DM'd him and he goes, "Shoot this girl an email. She will take care of you. She will hook it up. Magic@stardust. com."*

My tickets for that night, my second time seeing it and my first time seeing Lin, were prih-tee bomb ass. When I tell you they were the best fucking seats in the house—I was at the aisle, I was the second person in the bathroom, which, if you've ever seen a show at the Richard Rodgers you know is a BFD. The intermission bathroom lines, oy vey. I found out later that we were in the Obama seats. Yeah, I was sitting where President Barack Obama sat when he first saw the show! Can you say ballerrrrrrrrrrr?! I brought Rosa along again. We'd started this ride together and we were gonna go for another go-round together. There was nobody else I'd rather see *Hamilton* with again. We are soul sisters so I knew

---

* That obviously was not her email but it might as well have been.

she wouldn't judge me if/when I lost my shit again because I knew she'd be boo-hooing right along with me.

I decided to be bold and DM Lin. "I'm coming tonight, and I'm so excited to finally get to see you perform!" To my amazement, he wrote me back just minutes before the show started.

"Great, come backstage afterward!"

"Is he DMing you before the show?" Rosa asked incredulously.

"I'm that cool, homie."

Cool until I lost it again watching the magic for the second time. Rosa and I fell apart, again, at the *same* parts. The difference this time was we were smart and had stopped at Duane Reade beforehand to get tissues. The two girls sitting next to us were bawling, too, so we shared our bounty of Kleenex. We were veterans giving back.

"Girl, you don't even know," we warned the one closest to Rosa.

"I've seen it before!" she whispered through her sniffles.

So we weren't crazy! This is just what this show does to people. And trust me when I say it wasn't just the women in the audience that were moved to tears. It was amusing to see how some of the men tried to hide their emotions. There was the "stare at your feet as though you don't recognize the shoes you wore" strategy. The "cough and quickly wipe the tears with your fist before anyone sees the tears" trick. And my favorite (which I've employed myself), the "sit really still so as not to draw attention to the tears running past your cheeks and into the collar of your shirt" tactic. All valid attempts. All futile.

After the bows, Rosa and I went onstage again and I finally got to meet Lin. When he walked up to me and hugged me, it was as though we were grade-school friends who'd been separated because one of our families had moved cross-country but we'd stayed in touch all these years and FINALLY got to meet! (That's how it was for me, anyway. I'm pretty sure he's just that lovely to everyone.) I immediately teared up like the emotional sack that I am. I kind of made a REALLY big deal about how happy I was to finally meet him, and Oak—who had made it so I could actually get *in* to see the show—was like, "Just forget about me. That's cool . . . just tossed to the side." I told Oak he's family.*

I was so happy to finally see Lin as Hamilton. He was everything I'd hoped/wanted/expected him to be. He'd allowed me to feeeel for Hamilton, the eagerness, pride, success, failure, guilt, pain, despair, gratitude. I'd never been obsessed with anything or *anyone* like that in my life. I'd had Michael Jackson posters on my bedroom wall growing up, but it wasn't like I couldn't live without him, I'd never even gone to a concert. I watched Elvis movies every other weekend growing up, to the point my mother would look at me and be like, "This one and huh Elvis." I loved me some Elvis movies but I don't *own* a single film or album of his. I've never been a true fangirl about anything except maybe the Louis Vuitton Alma bag in vernis.† I have friends who are obsessed

---

* Oak and I have very similar backgrounds. We were both born in Newark, New Jersey, and are first-generation Americans of African parents. We practically *are* family.

† See addictions, chapter 2.

with a singer or band and find a way to see them whenever they're on tour, and I never really *got* it. I just never liked anything that much . . . until *Hamilton*. I now understand what theater-heads experienced when *Rent* went up. *Hamilton* is MY *Rent*. I had JUST seen it for the second time, and all I could think was . . . HOW DO I GET BACK? I knew I was being greedy. I didn't care. I. Was. Coming. Back.

I got invited to go to the Grammys that year. I said yes, not because the Grammys were cool and it was the best concert in town but because I knew, like everyone else, that *Hamilton* was gonna win for Best Musical Theater Album. I was most excited that the cast was to perform live for the broadcast. They weren't even going to be at Staples Center. They were performing via satellite from the Richard Rodgers. No matter. I was geeked to be "there." As excited for the win as someone who *actually* had something to do with the production. I saw a few weeks later on Snapchat that Daveed Diggs had people in his dressing room doing shots out of his Grammy while the rest of the group yelled, "Shots Out the Grammyyyyyy!" It looked glorious and I was totes jelly of every person who got to participate.

My birthday was coming up in April and I asked some friends to do a trip to New York to celebrate. My hope was to get us *Hamilton* tickets. They were more than aware of my Hamilmania and wanted to see what all the fuss was about. I emailed Oak's girl, Kaitlin, who said she couldn't promise anything but she'd get back to me. Two weeks later she blessed us with the news that we indeed had four tickets on the day before my birthday. Oh man, this was going to be the best birthday ever. We flew to New York and got connecting suites at the Gansevoort Park Hotel, which hooked us up with a birthday cake from a yummy bakery across the street and champagne. Two days before the show, on a little bubbly buzz, I wanted to DM Lin again to make sure he'd be in the show we were seeing. Cuz I was selfish and drunk like that.

I'm coming for my birthday my girls are in town! Wanted to see if you're performing.

No response. I felt a little queasy, like I'd crossed a line. I mean, I knew he had like, a billion things to do and people tugging at him from all directions. What made me think he was looking to keep me abreast of his performance schedule? I felt stupid. Then I realized he'd given me his cell number the last time I was in town. Whaaaaat? How did I not know I had a direct line? Foolish is how. I hesitated for one second, not wanting to be a stalker, but then I was like, FUCK IT and texted.

This time, he replied right away.

Yes so excited! Have something for you!

Pour moi? Little old moi?

We got to the show and had great seats again. We were buzzing with excitement when a lovely young lady leaned down and said, "Hi, Retta. I'm Kaitlin." Kaitlin! The sweet angel who had hooked me up with the tix this time *and* last. I was so excited to meet her. I told the girls who she was and they, too, were excited to meet the woman behind the gift. She said hi and told us to enjoy the show. Oh don't you worry, Kaitlin.

We will! No doubt in my mind. Well *most* of us were. Tej was upset that Leslie Odom Jr. was not performing that night.*

The show started and the fucking guy behind us started singing along, tapping his feet against my chair and giving commentary for his friend like it was a live version of *Mystery Fucking Science Theater 3000*. The fuck?? Oh hellz no. He was not about to ruin this experience for me. My friend Tina and I were so angry but couldn't say anything because, just before the show started, Tej had said hi to this guy. I didn't wanna make it weird for her by going off on him if this was a business colleague. I know people are excited to be there, hell, I had to force my*self* not to sing along. I curbed my shit because I knew how annoying it is and I wasn't looking to get cut by someone who'd paid two grand to see the show WITH-OUT my accompaniment. He finally caught on and shut the fuck up. I'm guessing it was all the obvious exhaling from the folks around him that got him to calm his ass down.

Intermission came and I looked over to my girls to see what they thought. Tej and Britnee were both tear-soaked.

"Omigod are y'all crying *already*??"

"I started crying in the opening number," Britnee said.

"I know. I just can't believe we're here," Tej could barely get out.

I laughed. If they cried through the first half, there was no way they would survive the second.

---

* I texted Leslie from the audience to let him know we were sad we weren't going to see him. He said he had just gotten back from his doctor and had a throat infection.

By the end of the show, as I expected, they were fucking broken. We made our way onstage and I again was in awe of this wonderful cast. Lin came over to me, wished me a happy birthday, and handed me a gift. It was a signed copy of *Hamilton: The Revolution*,* more affectionately known to superfans as *The Hamiltome*. It was the day before the official release date, April twelfth (my birthday), and I'd already preordered two copies that were being delivered to my house. He had signed it,

> *For Retta—*
> *Treat. Yo. Self.*
> *Siempre,*
> *Lin*

I'd already had the best birthday weekend with my girls, shopping and eating at great restaurants, and this was the icing on the dang cake.

When the Tonys came up in June, and *Hamilton* was nominated for sixteen awards, more than any other Broadway production in history, I was so happy for them. I literally have nothing to do with the show but it was very important to me to celebrate their Tony win(s). You didn't have to be psychic to know they were going to win. I wanted to be there for this moment. I wanted to go to the actual awards at the Beacon Theatre but was told, "You can't. Trust me, there is no room

---

* *Hamilton: The Revolution* is the book written by Lin and Jeremy McCarter chronicling the story of how *Hamilton* the Broadway smash came to be. It's a beautiful book, and the signed copy given to me by Lin is a prized possession.

in that building." Lucky for me I got an invite to the *Hamilton* party. Say word. Andrew Chappelle, who is a swing* in the show, requested that I get an invite and sure enough I did! I legit flew across the country for a party. I mean it wasn't just *any* party. It was the *Hamilton* Tony party at Tavern on the Green and I'm here to tell you it was worth it.

First off, Questlove was the DJ. If that's not an indication of how things were gonna go, I don't know what would be. There was food, drinks, drinks, and more drinks. I went with Rosa, duh, and got to hang with a new friend, Busy Phillips, who I had literally met through Snapchat. I congratulated Leslie and Lin on their wins and got to meet Lin's wife, Vanessa, who couldn't be lovelier.

"I feel like I know you!" I said.

"I know!" she said.

Oh gosh. She must've thought I was a stalker.

To clarify, I said, "I saw you on Rachael Ray!" Eesh, did that seem even more stalkerish? As obsessed with Lin, the genius behind my *Hamilton* obsession, as I was, it wasn't the I-want-to-steal-your-husband-away kind of love. I just think he's brilliant. I want his life to remain pristine. Him and his wife and his kids and his parents and family—I want everything to stay perfect and great 'til the end of time. I want each and every one of them to remain together and happy for as long as they all shall live. It's weird now that I read it but it's

---

* A swing is a member of the company/cast who understudies several chorus and/or dancing roles. If an understudy fills in for a lead role, a *swing* will act the parts normally performed by the understudy. As far as I'm concerned swings are the hardest-working folks in theater. They have to learn so many parts. I'd be scared shitless.

true. My friend Meredith has the same kind of love for President Obama. She thinks he's the most handsome and most charming, most loving, funny, generous man to walk this earth. I told her she sounded like she wanted to get in his pants. She said no, that she loves him *with* Michelle and wants him to stay with her forever and that they had the perfect family. I now get what she meant.

Now, you'd think I would've had my fill of *Hamilton* at this point. I'd seen it THREE times and got to celebrate the Tony success. You'd THINK . . . until I heard that Lin would be leaving the show. Lin, Leslie, and Phillipa Soo would be making their last appearance on the *Hamilton* stage on July 9, 2016. I wanted to go. I *had* to go. I had a serious conversation with myself: "It's ridiculous that you think you're going to go. There's no way." And then the little devil took over. *Just try. Just email Kaitlin. What could it hurt? The worst that could happen is she says, "No, not possible."* I knew it was probably a fucking shitshow with regard to ticket requests. I mean tickets for *weekday matinees* were impossible so tix for this LAST show were gonna be harder to get than seats next to Michelle at Obama's first inauguration. But you know what? You only live once. I said fuck it. I emailed her. "Is Rodgers sold out for Lin's last week?"

"Like you wouldn't believe. We might have a couple tix in the front mezz for his last night, but that's it . . ."

Wait, what? I might be able to go to that *last* performance. My heart started to race. My schedule was batshit crazy at the time. For one, I had just started working in earnest on *this* book and I had already made plans to go up to San Jose to watch the Sharks in the Stanley Cup finals. I couldn't afford another weekend out of town. But guess what . . . I figured that shit out.

I texted Tej to tell her the good news, then asked if she wanted to go since she didn't get to see Leslie the first time. She was IN. A few days later she sent me a text with a link to an article that said tickets to Lin's final show were selling for $20,000! You heard me right. Two-zero-zero-zero, and one more zero! That's MORE than a used Birkin bag. Wait, the Birkin has a utilitarian purpose and will be used for more than one night. That Birkin was becoming more of a steal than I THOUGHT! As far as I'm concerned I was saving money going on this trip cuz I promise you I spent nowhere near twenty grand . . . that's including airfare, room, tax, incidentals, AND any other expenses.

Tej and I flew out together and made a girl's weekend of it. We had tix to the closing night of *She Loves Me*, starring my friend Zac Levi, Laura Benanti, and Jane Krakowski. We made a reservation for dinner at legendary theater hangout Sardi's before the *Hamilton* performance. I was excited for it all. The afternoon before the show we had brunch with Andrew Chappelle, Oak, and Kaitlin, better known as my #HamilAngels. They talked about a big after-party for Lin thrown by his father. Kaitlin said she'd have invited me but had no control over the guest list.

"You can be my plus-one," Oak said to me.

You guys. I mean. It was almost too much.

And when I tell you that Lin's last show was epic. If I thought the energy in the room was electric the previous time I had seen it, *this* night it was off the charts. You couldn't help but feel like your molecules were buzzing knowing you got into the room where it was happening on this night. We were all looking around trying to remember every single thing about this moment.

First off, I saw Rosie O'Donnell in the lobby. I'd seen her on *The Late Late Show with James Corden* when, at the time, she had seen *Hamilton* twelve times. This was to be her twenty-fourth viewing. Yeah. Insert wide-eyed emoji HERE! I said hi to her and I'm sure she thought, *I don't know you but "Hey."* I felt we shared an obsession and that if she did know me she'd get me. Other celebs to score these precious tickets were J.Lo with her twins and signif other at the time, Casper Smart; my friends Troy Garity and his wife, Simone Bent, and his mom; Jane Fonda; Charlie Rose; Spike Lee; Mariska Hargitay and Peter Hermann*; and one John Kerry, who created a surprising amount of curiosity among the night's patrons.

When the lights went down the crowd erupted. It was about to begin. Leslie began the opening as he had so many times before, but this time he walked onto stage like a man who knew he had done his job and had done it well. When he got to the line, "Get your education, don't forget from whence you came, and the world is gonna know your name. What's your name, man?" Lin made his entrance. When he sang "Alexander Hamilton" the crowd started an applause that lasted a full minute. I don't know how Lin didn't lose it cuz *I* did. The rest of the night was charged with an emotion you can only imagine.

---

* Peter appears in one of my favorite episodes of *30 Rock*, where he dates Liz Lemon only to find out they're cousins. He's sooo charming and the familial realization brings me to tears EVERY time. Genius.

I remember our last week shooting *Parks*. Every day was charged with emotion as, one by one, cast members had their series wrap. The last to wrap was Amy, and it brought tears to our eyes (especially Jim cuz he's a big baby and cries at everything). Saying good-bye to seven years of work that garnered familial feelings toward the people around you. It's the kind of emotion that makes it hard to function. *That* is the emotion I can only imagine he was going through . . . and he still had two and a half hours of show to do.

When Leslie performed "In the Room Where It Happens" it was like I'd never seen him before, and the crowd awarded him for it. The applause was loud, long, and heartfelt. Rory O'Malley, who had had his first performance as the king on the night my friends and I attended for my birthday, played the monarch with such whimsy that it brought such joy to us, his subjects. Chris Jackson was feeling the feels, too. I imagine it was hard to perform for the last time with his bestie. One of my favorite moments was when Oak came onstage as Madison after "It's Quiet Uptown" and was way more choked up than I remember him in the previous two times I had seen him play the ex-president. Phillipa Soo . . . what can I say about Phillipa Soo other than she broke me for one last time. Her final number, the *show's* final number, was just . . . heavy. So, so heavy. She was a fucking trooper, getting through it without collapsing.

The curtain call was another exercise in stillness and composure. The audience once again gave each performer their due praise. My hands hurt I clapped so hard. And at this point I feel it's probably moot to point out I was hardly dry-eyed. Once we pulled ourselves together, Tej and I made our way to the stage for one final round of after-show kudos. Onstage I got to chat with my friends Troy and Simone. There were so many people onstage it was difficult to see who of the cast was still there. Obviously everyone wanted to share their love and appreciation for what they had given us. I finally saw Daveed in the crowd. I walked over to him to tell him he was great *as usual* and that the only thing I regretted was having never participated in "Shots Out the Grammy!"

"Oh snap! Let's go do it right now!"

He proceeded to yell for Oak to join us. I was so geeked I didn't know what to do with myself. On the way to the production office where the Grammys were being stored, Oak stopped near a white-haired woman with a friendly smile and asked, "Retta, do you know who this is?" I assumed she was either a liberal arts professor of some sort or an award-winning poet. She had that look about her. I sheepishly replied, "I don't," to which he replied, "This is Daveed's mom!" I was like, "Heyyyyyyyy!" I was thrilled to meet her and thought she was the cutest thing.

"Wait, *you're* Retta? You're great at Twitter."

Shut the front door. Daveed's mom was familiar with my Twitter game. Hahahaha. That small acknowledgment brought me a disproportionate amount of pride. We all went into the production office along with Tej, Seth Stewart, and a few others. Barbara (Daveed's mom), Seth, and I did "Shots Out the Grammy!" It was epic and it was more than I could've asked for on this night.

The after-party was at the Renaissance New York Times Square Hotel. I got a drink at the bar and ran into Barbara who, at this point, I was calling Babs. She joined me on a bench against a window. The party attendees were having a great time and I watched from the side. Lin walked over and we got to chat for a moment. It wasn't a long chat, but I remember feeling that it, oddly, gave me some closure on this fangirl experience that had been so foreign to me and yet so all-encompassing. I got to have my closure with *Hamilton*. From the time I downloaded that soundtrack up until the time I was lucky enough to see the show for the fourth time, I'd listened to the album Every. Single. Day. On my phone, in my car, while cleaning my house, before I went to sleep.

After a yearlong fixation, it was time to move on.

I still keep in touch with some of the cast, like Oak and Andrew. Lin sent me a friend request on Facebook. Like a geek, I screen-grabbed it and sent it to my friends. At first, I was afraid to accept it because as much as I feel like we're totes besties and of course should be FB friends, I felt I *didn't* want him to know my foolishness. I didn't want him to see my page and be like, "Retta posts a lot about *Hamilton*. Yikes. This bitch is crazy."

PLUS, I know one day they *will* make a movie version of *Hamilton*. You never know. It's not beyond the realm of believability that they'd consider a plus-size Angelica. And if I get that call from my manager . . .

"This is big. This is *really* big."

You better believe I'm showing up for that shit. I'm not going to make that mistake twice.

This time, I'll bring my flats.*

---

* It's August 2017 and I am copy editing this book and thought I'd add that I went to the Los Angeles opening of *Hamilton* at The Pantages. It was my sixth viewing of the show, as I had seen it a few months ago in Chicago. *Now* I can let it go.

Which Came First? The Chicken, OBVI*

I'm driving up to Sacramento, a five-and-a-half-hour trip, and the entire time I'm craving KFC.

I'm black.

So once I hit the city limits, I stop at the first Kentucky Fried Chicken that I see, I go in, I give my order.

"I'll have a three-piece chicken with biscuit, original recipe, dark meat." You see, white meat does nothing for me, it's just too dryyy. "I'll have some grape jelly and some hot sauce, please."

"We ain't got no chicken."

"Excuse me?"

---

* This is my chicken bit. It is the first professional joke I ever wrote. I am eternally proud of it because I wrote it twenty years ago and this motherfucker still hits. And as a lazy writer (see chapter 8), it is the jewel in my stand-up crown.

"We'ze outta chicken."

How is it possible that Kentucky Fried Chicken would run out of Kentucky. Fried. Chicken? I'm sorry, was today's shipment hijacked? Or did someone decide during your Monday morning meeting that chicken's just not the way to go? So you're telling me: What we have is an establishment whose name is essentially "chicken" but you ain't got no chicken. That's like going to Victoria's Secret and they tell you, "I'm sorry, ma'am, but we'ze outta drawers."

So I'm like, "This is KFC, right?"

"Yeah, but we ain't got no chicken."

"Well, Slim, what *do* you have?"

"We got the corn bread. We got the biscuits. We got dem sides. We DO have that chicken sammitch."

Sammitch.

Did you just say SAM-MITCH? What is a chicken *sammitch*, cuz I don't see it on the menu. Now, I was tempted to ask Mr. Phonetically Challenged if when he goes to a Mexican restaurant does he often order the chicken *fuh-jiht-uhs*. But I held my tongue. I did say, however:

"Look here . . . Anfernee? Anferneeeeee, I came to Kentucky Fried . . . *Chicken* so that I might partake in some Kentucky. Fried. *Chicken*. Now somebody behind that counter's gon' get me some damn *chicken*. I don't care if it's you, or Sam, or Mitch, or the Colonel himself, with his white-suit-wearin', goatee-sportin', walkin'-stick totin', country-country twang-twang accent-havin' wrinkled ass, you better make like Nike and just do it. Otherwise you're going to experience what it's like when a large irritable black woman is dissatisfied with her service. I just drove five and one half hours with nothing on my mind but a three-piece chicken and biscuit. So I'm not leaving here without a little red-and-white box that's got two thighs and a leg. If it's got to be yo' two thighs and a leg, so be it. But I would suggest you hop your narrow ass over to the supermarket and make friends with somebody in that poultry department."

Now, needless to say, they did what they could to keep me content. I left Kentucky Fried Chicken an hour later with a complimentary bucket of *Perdue* chicken, fried and rotisserie, a dozen biscuits, a gallon of sweet tea, two chicken sammitches, and a whole lot of potato wedges.

Oh, and Anfernee? He carried it to my car.

Acknowledgments

Thanks to my parents, without whom I would not be. You gave me life, a moral center, and I respect and honor you for it. Thank you for loving and providing for me even though money doesn't grow on trees.

To my brothers George and Mich: I love you even when you annoyed the shit outta me. You make me laugh! And to your sig nifs, Brenda and April, thank you for loving these boys and giving me my beyond adorable, sweet and loving nephews Andrew, George, Brendan, and the almost-here Justice. They bring endless joy. Thanks for putting up with my incessant FaceTimes so that I may see their faces.

My cousins Siah & Sonnie: I love y'all.

Thanks to Quressa Robinson for asking that I do this book. I always thought I might write a book one day but because of you it's a reality.

Mad love to JL Stermer for holding my hand during the book proposal process and when I was feeling overwhelmed and wanted to quit, for suggesting that I "just see if they'd give me an offer." Holy shit, I can't believe that shit worked! You're the best, mamma.

Thank you to Dibs for the many hours of sitting together/ Skyping in order to pull these stories out of me. For laughing at my silliness and engaging me so that I would remember these stories. For taking my verbal vomit and putting them in some sensible order. You for sure did the lion's share of handholding and I appreciate you for it.

Thanks to Paul Fedorko for coming on to the project and dealing with the stuff I didn't know how or want to do. And to Chloe Rabinowitz for handling the minutia. The Getty Images situation alone could've put me into an asylum.

Thanks to Elizabeth Beier for also coming on and making a smooth transition for me, and to Nicole Williams for staying on top of what I needed to turn in and when.

Thank you to the dear Jaime Elyse, who made my dress for this cover. You are a dream. I love your energy and appreciate that you are so giving of your time and talent.

To my team: Sam, Jason, Aron, Ali, and Jordan. You guys are the shit. I appreciate all your encouragement and all the fighting you do for me. I especially appreciate how pissed you get (looking at you, Sam) when you feel I am not being treated fairly/respected for what I bring to the table. It allows me to NOT have to cut muhfuhkuhs.

To my forever champion young Tej. I love that you get my foolishness and indulge my far-reaching wants and needs. There has never been an offer to do something that you haven't told me I'd be great in. I often beg to differ but I love that you insist that I will kill it. Remember when we had our girls' trip to NY for Hamilton? GOOD TIMES!

Thank you to America Ferrara, Amy Poehler, Aziz Ansari, and Lena Dunham for reading the first five chapters early on and being so kind with their blurbs. I respect and appreciate y'all so much.

Thanks to the incomparable Lin-Manuel Miranda for his

genius and for creating my first true theatrical obsession. It's been over a year since I fell in love with this work and it STILL makes me feel some kind of way. I appreciate that you've been so kind and indulged my gushing and light stalking. As much as I love *Hamilton*, I love introducing people to it and having them thank ME (as if) for their new love. You are a gift. And to the HamFam that I have gotten to know and love, including Okieriete "Oak" Onaodowan, Andrew Chappelle, Daveed Diggs, Alex Lacamoire, Kaitlin Fine, Dylan Pager, Sasha Hutchings, and Miguel Mediola. Thanks to the many iterations of the cast for making one of my most fulfilling obsessions, and to Oak, Daveed, and Andrew for remaining friends even after you saw how *Hamil*-crazed I was. I would do shots out the Grammy with you any day.

To my *Parks & Rec* cast: I love you all and I love that we continue to share our lives with one another via our Parks Fam group text. Thanks to Mike Schur and Greg Daniels for allowing me to be a part of this sweet and inspiring show and gifting me with Amy, Aubrey, Rashida, Nick, Aziz, Chris, Adam, and Jim! Shawna Malwae TWEEP! Shawna Malwae Twee-ee-eep! #DarkParks

And as much as I credit my parents for making me the person that I am, I must also credit my friends. While Debbie and George laid down the foundation, my friends have helped shape the most current version of me. Love to my ride-or-dies: Rosa, Sandi, Britzee, T-Mobile, Kimba, MereBear, Laura, Cindo, Heather, Nam, Shaliseets, Nay, Lex, and Mogo.